The 10 Principles of the Feminine

How to Embrace Feminine Energy and Find the Power Within

The 10 Principles of the Feminine

How to Embrace Feminine Energy and Find the Power Within

Roxana Dragusel

BOOKS

Winchester, UK
Washington, USA

JOHN HUNT PUBLISHING

First published by O-Books, 2023
O-Books is an imprint of John Hunt Publishing Ltd., 3 East St., Alresford,
Hampshire SO24 9EE, UK
office@jhpbooks.com
www.johnhuntpublishing.com
www.o-books.com

For distributor details and how to order please visit the 'Ordering' section on our website.

Text copyright: Roxana Dragusel 2022

ISBN: 978 1 80341 309 9
978 1 80341 310 5 (ebook)
Library of Congress Control Number: 2022911652

A CIP catalogue record for this book is available from the British Library.

Design: Stuart Davies

UK: Printed and bound by CPI Group (UK) Ltd, Croydon, CR0 4YY
Printed in North America by CPI GPS partners

We operate a distinctive and ethical publishing philosophy in all areas of our business, from our global network of authors to production and worldwide distribution.

Contents

To: Laura and Ileana,
for having initiated me
into the secrets of the Universe

Preface

It was on a New Year's Day that I started to write this book, as a symbol of a new phase of my earthly journey. I have always found that it is a good omen to start the year in writing.

> *In the beginning was the Word, and the Word was with God, and the Word was God.*

May the words in this book also alchemize in you a new beginning of a journey to authenticity and personal power, and an initiation into what feminine energy truly is. For there can be no light without darkness and no masculine without feminine, and we must all learn to balance both aspects within us before we can step into our highest potential as human beings.

Introduction

Much has been written lately on the divine masculine and feminine as the highest expressions of the divine in duality, residing within all forms of life. It is not the purpose of this book to provide an in-depth analysis of these concepts, nor to focus on the philosophical aspect of them, but rather to provide a practical and pragmatic understanding of what exactly it is in us all that we call *feminine*, and how we can use its qualities and attributes to harness the full potential of the resources within us.

This book is addressed to both men and women, since feminine energy resides in all of us (although it might be expressed in diverse ways, depending on the gender we adhere to or on the general and socially acceptable definitions of them). I find that oftentimes we fall into the trap of semantics and fail to go beyond actual terms and definitions, therefore I would like to point out that the concepts outlined in this book go beyond gender, sexual orientation, or any social and religious norms we may choose to follow.

In a modern word which pushes us to adapt in order to survive, where gender equity and freedom of expression might blur the lines between what we consider masculine and feminine, I often see women nowadays enquiring on how it is that they can be more feminine and men asking how they can express a healthier self, beyond the aggressive type of masculinity they have been raised with. For those of you who find themselves in either of the above categories, this is a read which might provide you with some answers. It is not to say that this should become the norm in the area of personal and interpersonal development, but these are examples of how different people might choose to express themselves in a more authentic way, as opposed to what they were conditioned to be, believe or aspire to.

I felt compelled to write about the feminine, rather than the masculine, because I feel that it is both misunderstood and ignored. There are a lot of misconceptions related to it, such as that being feminine means displaying certain external characteristics related to looks and clothing, or being a mother, and while these can certainly be expressions of the feminine, they are just a small fraction of it. There are other more impactful ways in which feminine energy expresses itself, so if one does not relate to the above it does not mean that they cannot be feminine. Equally, displaying feminine characteristics is uncomfortable and sometimes repulsive to men, because they are also biased by these misconceptions, and it is important to point out that the feminine and the masculine do not exclude, but complete each other. A man lacking feminine energy, as well as a woman lacking masculine energy, would not be able to maintain a healthy relationship with themselves and others, let alone be happy and fulfilled. There is a need in all of us to express and honor our feminine energy and it is necessary to first become aware of this, and secondly to choose those manners of expression which are suited to us, and not those which are defined by social norms (which leads to us being unhappy because we are trying to fit into a character that does not suit us).

The ten principles of the feminine, which I felt guided to share with you, will hopefully shed some light on how exactly feminine energy presents itself in our lives and how we can better identify it, connect with it and use it for our benefit and the benefit of those around us. There is much more to feminine energy than what is written in this book, not to mention that masculine energy would also deserve a book of its own. At the same time, a lot of principles outlined here, especially the more abstract ones, such as the energetic body or God or the Akashic field, are grossly simplified for the sake of clarity. The understanding of these concepts, self-awareness and spirituality are all processes that take time, and as with all learning processes, they should flow from simple to complex (in order to gain an understanding of calculus, one must first learn subtraction and division, which although much simpler, do not necessarily hold less value). And when reaching a superior understanding of these concepts, you might realize that they are all just steppingstones, and that is not to say that they stop being valid, but rather that their importance and the way you approach them change along the way. So, the only requirement of this book would be to have an open mind; choosing to stay with subtractions and divisions because they are reliable and clear is a perfectly valid choice, as long as you can accept that there is truth beyond them as well.

While discovering the concepts that I describe here, you will realize that you might be more familiar with some aspects of the feminine, and more comfortable with them, while other aspects will seem more foreign. This is not unusual, and it is not a reason to perceive it as a negative evaluation of the self or of certain behaviors, but a chance to look at things from another perspective and to grow, even if that growth just means appreciating yourself more. If you do not resonate with some of the ideas, or are not ready to embrace them, make a mental note and save them for later, when they will be of use. Regardless of gender, the behaviors and expressions outlined here are basic human experiences, but understanding why and how they pertain to your feminine aspect can help you accept them and relate to them easier, and ultimately know yourself better.

A Few Considerations on the Yin-Yang Concept

The concept of yin and yang has its base in the old Chinese school of philosophy and cosmology and dates back to the 3rd century BC. It refers to the idea that the Universe is composed of opposites which both antagonize and complement each other, none being able to exist without its counterpart, for instance light and dark, young and old, truth and deception, feminine and masculine. It is not that one is better than the other, but that one needs the other in order to define itself (just like in order to define something as being small or big, there is a need for a standard of comparison). So, there is nothing better than the concept of yin and yang to explain the idea that everything is relative, and the dynamic between these two opposite forces maintains balance in the Universe.

In terms of this philosophy, the feminine represents the yin, while the masculine represents the yang, and these are two aspects that reside at all levels of creation, from the large cosmic structures to the individual atom, and are therefore also applicable to humans and any other living beings. The yang would include attributes such as light, heat, energetic, external, loud, etc., while the yin would include the opposite: shade, cold, calm, internal, quiet. At the level of the human being, this concept also translates into the existence of two opposite genders, each displaying characteristics of its own nature. I would point out, though, that pertaining to one gender from the physical or biological perspective does not necessarily determine one's nature in terms of the yin-yang principle; for instance someone can be a woman but display more yang than yin attributes (be more masculine than feminine).

Although not an exhaustive list, examples of characteristics residing in the masculine spectrum of energy are having direction, ambition, logical thinking, leadership, autonomy, risk taking, planning, organizing, setting boundaries, seeing the big picture, protecting, providing and giving. On the other hand, feminine qualities are feeling, flowing, allowing, being intuitive, nurturing, compassionate, connecting to others, communicating, creating, having attention to details, empathy, healing, receiving. However, in the yin-yang diagram, which you can find in the preface of this book, it is obvious that there is always some yin in the yang (the black dot in the white half), and vice versa, so humans will also display some of the characteristics of the opposite gender. Needless to say, we must be able to display both in order to face life in a healthy and balanced way, although we might not display them continuously or with the same intensity every time.

When I say that we should strive for a balance between the feminine and the masculine aspects of ourselves, it does not necessarily mean that this is a 50-50 matter, although it might, if this is your natural expression of self. Human beings are born unique, and this uniqueness may manifest in having very different proportions of the above, regardless of the gender they are assigned to at birth. In other words, some women might naturally express more feminine energy than others and so can men (without necessarily failing to be 'manly' in the general understanding of the term, if this is what they resonate with). The only problem arises when society and sometimes even you seek to change this natural pattern in order to fit into a persona or lifestyle which might be considered by others to be pleasant, successful or appropriate. This is when you lose your true identity and sense of self, and inevitably become confused, unfulfilled or even depressed. So the challenge, should you choose to accept it, is to get your natural resources back and remember who you truly are, so that you can grow into what you were born to be, rather than what you are expected to.

A Few Considerations on the Multidimensionality of the Human Being

Being multidimensional means being composed of several different pieces which do not connect on the same level, but rather overlap one another, not much different from a building with multiple storeys. The ground floor, in the case of a human being, would be represented by its physical aspect, meaning the physical body. This is not the only piece in the puzzle, but we might be tempted to believe so because it is the only one we can perceive with our five senses. Sometimes, people also believe that they have a soul (and this is especially the case of religious people), so they believe that there is an additional floor above, but for some reason they also believe there is no elevator to take them there, at least not before their existence on Earth has ended. I have yet to see a building or any other construction with several levels where one cannot move up and down, and I also do not see the purpose of such a building.

In addition to the soul, which is the energetic body, there are also other bodies, among which the most important are the mental and the emotional. They all serve different purposes and they complete each other, and even though we might not feel them, they are there. These are not necessarily separated from each other, but as I mentioned they are simply different dimensions of ours. Out of all, the energetic body is the one which persists beyond time and space (so it is eternal), while the mental and emotional bodies are there to support the physical body during our existence on the physical plane. Also, the energetic body is always connected with the ones of other beings, in other words there is no individuality on the energetic level, but only on the other levels. While we might live as individuals for some part of our existence, we are, beyond this, timeless and formless beings always connected to the

Source which is generating them, or God if this is a concept you resonate with. So if you would be able to see your soul, hypothetically, it would not look like a spectre with a human figure as sometimes depicted in movies and cartoons, but you would not even be able to distinguish it from the souls of other beings. The whole Universe, at an energetic level, looks like an infinite spiderweb from which filaments emerge continuously, forming life and experiencing it by giving birth to matter.

Having said that, there is a possibility to experience our other dimensions while living in a physical body, but since our physical brain only forms after conception, it is natural that it does not contain any memories or information from before. We not only exist after our physical life, but also before, and I am highlighting it because even religions that promote the belief that we have an immortal soul fail to educate on what precedes our physical existence. Talking about the afterlife is all very well, but how about the *beforelife*? So in order to experience our soul and our permanence as beings we cannot rely on our logical brain, but we can become aware of the connection our physical body has with its subtler forms, and before doing so we should first understand what energy is and how to identify it. This book is focused on feminine energy because it is She that allows us to feel this connection. If we refer to the example of the building, feminine energy would be like an elevator allowing us to explore our other storeys, so understanding it is a major step in discovering our true self.

Chapter 1

Attraction

The science of allowing the Universe in

Feminine energy is by definition pointed inwards, as opposed to masculine energy which flows outwards. This means that it acts as a magnet for things and people to come into our life and proximity, in other words it is the domain of manifestation without effort, and most of the time, without intent. It is not to say that it is pointless and purely coincidental, but it allows the Universe to express itself through us, unrestricted by imposed boundaries or wishes derived from the ego and expectations. This chapter is not a manual on how to use the Law of Attraction as it is understood in modern society, but it does explain to a certain extent how it is intended to work.

When I say that the Universe manifests itself in an unrestricted way, I am referring to the way objects, events and other beings are effortlessly allowed to come into our life without expectation of how and when they should present themselves. Most of us want to manifest a specific job, lifestyle or person in our reality without asking ourselves if this is truly what we need or whether it is the best thing for us. By *knowing* what we want at any time point in our existence, we are implying that there can be no greater good or blessing in our life than what we can imagine. The problem with imagination is that it is always limited by our own experience and perhaps our brain capacity (without giving it any negative connotation, we must admit that some people certainly have a better or richer imagination than others). Our own planet is a particularly good example of how nature can do much better than humans in this respect. If we think of the variety of life forms around us and how intricate and surprising some of them are, it is difficult to believe that a human being could have ever designed, at least some of them, out of pure imagination. Moreover, most of what has ever been created in the artistic space is merely an imitation of what we see around us, whether it is a landscape painting, the colors we use or the shape of objects we create. With few exceptions there is very little out there which exceeds nature's expectations.

The reason the Law of Attraction does not work for some people or in certain cases, is because we are too specific in what it is that we want to achieve. While there is energy around us which wants to flow towards us (money, people, opportunities, are all different expressions of the same energy, and can be more or less physical), there is no space inside us to receive it because it is already taken by our expectations. By being overly rigid in what we want to achieve, we are not allowing this flow of energy. I am sure that all of us have had at least one instance of disappointment in our past, for not getting *the* job, *the* lover, *the* house we wanted.

While it is perfectly natural and beneficial to want certain things (as opposed to being completely passive and not wanting to create or achieve anything), we must keep in mind that some of those things and people might not want us back. You will say that it is ridiculous to believe that a house or a car have a will of their own (which it is), but as mentioned before they are just physical manifestations of energy. And energy does have a will of its own, in the sense that it flows and functions according to very well-established universal laws, therefore one does not bend the Universe but rather allows itself to be filled by it.

Instead of wanting to create a very specific thing, ask yourself what is it that wants to be created through you and allow it to happen. Sometimes it might be exactly what you would have expected or wanted, and sometimes it might not. Introspection is a great tool to unravel what it is inside of us that wants to come out, and so are meditation, energy work and, surprisingly, connecting and exchanging ideas with people around us. I say it is surprising because the stimulus seems to be coming from outside in this example, but I found that very often some people strike a chord inside of us, allowing a certain idea or creation to take form in an unexpected moment. We call these people healers (contrary to the ordinary understanding of the term, a healer is not a medical professional, nor a spiritual practitioner – although both can be true in certain cases, but someone who helps us get our power or identity back). From this respect anyone can be a healer and this is, as mentioned before, a feminine quality. Not surprisingly, like attracts like, so this feminine quality attracts more of the same in ourselves and others, such as creativity.

Another way of allowing the Law of Attraction to work for us is by identifying what it is that makes us happy or fulfilled, or what we are particularly good at (most of the time, if we are good at something we also enjoy it and the other way around). Once identified, practice it in whatever way or to whatever extent possible, but without having a specific expectation to get something out of it or with a hidden agenda of financial gain. Money may come out of it, as it often does, but it is a limiting belief to think that whatever talent we have, whether it is artistic, technical or vocational, can and should result in financial abundance. It is not about attracting abundance by what you like doing, but about putting in motion a flow of energy that can result in unexpected things; allowing this unexpectedness is what attraction is all about. Very often it attracts self-confidence, relaxation, joy, and these are in themselves powerful tools to work with and to ultimately attract abundance for instance, if this is what we are looking for.

People who exert more feminine energy are more allowing of this unexpectedness to come into their lives. If we think about a couple who expect a baby or want to conceive, although it might seem like a naïve example but for the sake of clarity please allow me to refer to it – we often hear the father-to-be expressing a wish that the child might be of this or that gender, whereas the mother would rather say, "I don't care what it is, as long as it is healthy." The reverse might happen if the polarities of the couple are inverted and the mother exerts more masculine energy, which is in no way unusual or unhealthy, it just means that her partner might have more feminine energy in order to balance the dynamic of the couple.

Now that we have come to the topic of romantic partnerships, I would like to illustrate how attraction works in the setting of interpersonal relationships.

As mentioned in the beginning of this chapter, feminine energy is pointed inwards and masculine energy is pointed outwards. It is not by coincidence that the human reproductive organs display the same characteristics. Therefore, attraction is primarily a feminine principle. Without any reference to gender, it is safe to say that the feminine is the one which attracts the masculine and not the other way around. You will argue perhaps that masculine features are also attractive (and they are, to both the same and the opposite gender), but even though a man for instance might express very masculine characteristics, the quality of attracting, of being attractive, is a feminine quality in itself. It is a good illustration of how opposite energies blend within a person, although it is either not obvious or it goes unobserved and taken for granted.

This polarity determines the natural dynamic of the chaser and the chased, if we are to grossly simplify the complex interaction between two people. Also for the sake of clarity, I might refer to heterosexual couples but you will find that the same dynamic is expressed in couples of the same gender, since there will always be manifestations of both energies in any couple. This is obvious when we think about the traditional, apparently old-fashioned types of courtship where it is generally argued that the man should be doing the chasing. It is not old fashioned, but it merely reflects the natural dance of polar energies as explained above. It just so happens that traditionally, men displayed more masculine energy and women expressed more feminine energy (whether by nature or by social conditioning, is another topic which I will not discuss here).

So, if you wish to improve the quality of relationships in your life, evaluating where you stand on the spectrum of masculine-feminine, regardless of your gender, is a good starting point. Do you naturally enjoy approaching people, being the one who initiates contact of any kind (in other words being on the giving side), or do you prefer being approached (being on the receiving side)? Or have you been conditioned to act in opposition to your own nature because this is what was considered appropriate in your family or community? Of course, it might be unhealthy to choose one side and always stick to it regardless of the circumstances. But I think it is safe to state that people will act out of their primary energy mostly and in usual circumstances.

As a disclaimer to what is written above, you should remember that the principle of attraction per se is not intended towards a specific goal or person, but as mentioned before it allows the right energy to come into manifestation. In other words, trying to attract a very specific person, and only that one, might result in very disappointing experiences, since it limits the spectrum of possibilities of what you can attract. Being in love and hoping for reciprocity is natural, but obstinately trying to attract a specific person who does not reciprocate often results in complete failure and in the belief that there is no such thing as the Law of Attraction because it does not work. So allow the Universe to surprise you, or God, depending on which concept you resonate with.

On the same topic of polarity, we have all heard the saying *opposites attract*. Having said that, if what you are attracting does not feel right, if the relationships in your life are not fulfilling to you, then perhaps you are not acting out of your natural energy and therefore are attracting the opposite of what you actually need. I see this in women, more often than I would like to, that being conditioned to be independent, self-reliant, career-oriented has resulted in the fact that the woman is no longer in tune with her feminine energy and displays an entire range of oddly masculine behaviors which in turn lead to broken relationships and grief, and sometimes even aggressiveness. Such women have issues attracting the right partner or often any type of partner, because their level of attractiveness is diminished. When I say *attractiveness*, I am not referring to any physical or mental attributes, but to the energetic principle of attraction.

On the other hand, it is just as true that some women are naturally born with higher levels of masculine energy, and they will easily thrive in environments where masculine qualities are highly valued, such as a business community or a highly technical or scientific one. They will also not have any issues finding the right partner, because they will most likely not feel the need to attract in a receptive way, but they would rather act on their masculine energy and initiate or do the chasing.

So it is not about how you *should* behave in terms of social norms but about how it *feels* natural to behave when you are authentic and true to yourself. Same goes for choosing the right profession or career path.

As already described, the quality of being attractive is primarily energetic and not physical, contrary to the modern definition of the term. It is someone's vibe or aura that sparks an interest and magnetizes, and not necessarily their physical aspect. This explains why we might meet people who are considered to be physically attractive by the general standard but to whom we do not feel particularly attracted. It is not to say that the physical aspect is unimportant or that it should be disregarded, but it is only a fraction of what generates attraction.

Choosing a partner primarily on the basis of physical characteristics usually results in dramatic or short-termed relationships or flings, which is not surprising considering that although there might be some physical or physiological incentives to it, there is no real attraction in the couple. It is what we learn with great despair in our teenage years when we first find ourselves interested romantically in people. Unfortunately, some remain stuck in this pattern of relating even in their late adult years, and as incredible as it might seem, it also constitutes a basis for choosing a spouse or life partner for these people. I can imagine that while reading this, some of you might think that it is immature and that it seldom happens with adults, and I even hear some of you saying, "I don't do that!" But, if you are to be honest with yourself, have you actually given a good thought to what exactly it is that attracts you in a person? And above all, what is it exactly that you are looking for in a partner? In case you did take the time to answer this second question, I am certain that most of you have hardly put any physical attributes on the list. So it is advisable to make your own list and become aware of this aspect before allowing yourself to be unconsciously pulled into a relationship over someone's physical appearance.

Very feminine women are usually also considered very attractive, but again it is the quality of having feminine energy which is responsible for magnetizing masculine energy, more than the physical aspect. The same holds true for men; if a man has the ability to magnetize people from across the room (think about a movie star, a public person or very charismatic one), it is because they have also cultivated some form of feminine energy, consciously or not. It is not by accident that artists attract so much attention on themselves; being in the media might be a contributing factor, but they would surely also exhibit a lot of creativity, the ability to communicate and connect authentically with others or they are simply funny or playful (all of these being feminine qualities). Masculine energy on the other hand has no need to attract, it just *does*, it is an active force rather than a passive, receptive one, and has no interest in how others react to it, because it doesn't *feel*. Consequently, men who are disconnected from their feminine side are often perceived as being bullies or insensitive and are unable to form healthy and long-lasting connections, and might eventually end up being considered repelling.

So to close this topic of attraction, although you will find further reference to it throughout the book, I would summarize the take-home message and the main ideas that should be kept in mind before diving further in the mysteries of the Law of Attraction, should you wish to do so.

- Everything in this Universe is either energy or a condensed form of energy.
- Attraction is an open principle; it graciously allows in whatever there is that needs to come in, without judgement and restriction.
- Feminine energy is responsible for magnetizing. The more feminine energy one holds, the more attractive capacity they will have.
- Interpersonal attraction functions on the basis of polarity: the feminine aspects in one will attract the masculine aspects in another.

Chapter 2

Manifestation

The domain of creation and of bringing the formless into form

We have spoken about the principle of attraction in a very descriptive way, and you may ask yourselves what the difference is between attraction and manifestation, as these two terms are commonly interchanged or misunderstood.

Manifestation has a more factual aspect to it and it doesn't only reside in the feminine spectrum of energy by requiring creativity, but also in the masculine one. It can be said that manifestation is a more structured and intended type of attraction or that attraction is the first stage of manifestation. Attracting things might sometimes be easier than maintaining them because the latter also requires some sort of planning or consistency. If we think about the nature around us, we see that everything that comes to life has a very definite and clear structure which allows it to persist beyond birth, whether this is a certain biological mechanism or a chemical structure which allows it to endure the test of time. Who and what determines this structure? It is hard to say, and scholars, scientists and mystics have taken turns throughout the known history to explain or clarify the mystery of how matter is structured in the Universe. In any case, it is safe to say that some forces and laws have been identified, which although do not provide the full picture, certainly help understand up to a certain point how matter manifests itself.

The realm of structure and of law is a masculine one, therefore it makes sense that you should learn how to master your masculine energies as well before becoming properly acquainted and comfortable with manifesting, whether that is a business, a family, your dream life, or anything else you might feel called to create.

So manifestation belongs to both the masculine and the feminine in equal proportions.

Firstly, to try and clarify the energetic mechanisms of manifestation we should provide a proper definition of the term. Manifestation is the ability to attract and maintain form coming from the realm of the formless, with the help of intent and of creativity. Therefore, creativity is both a means and a purpose, which is not surprising since all creation is composed of different smaller parts which represent creations themselves: fibers, molecules, atoms, subatomic particles, which are nothing but energy recycled from other forms of energy in the Universe. Without wanting to reduce everything to the issue of the chicken or the egg, it is good to keep in mind that in order to create we must use tools that are given to us or that have been manifested before. In other words, being conscious and aware of what it is that we have at our disposal is imperative in order to create something.

To translate the above in more practical terms, knowing ourselves, our abilities and our talents and identifying what we can take from our environment to create something is a first step in manifestation. The question is: are we aware enough or present enough to actually see inside and outside of us or are we just moving through life in a half-asleep state, mechanically doing and repeating what we see around us? And if we are able to see, do we actually appreciate all these things or is it that we take them for granted or underestimate them?

So if I were to summarize what it is that we need in order to start creating something in the first place, it would be intent (be aware that you wish to manifest something and be clear about what that is) and resource (learn to identify and value what it is in you that can constitute a resource: a skill, a talent, a certain piece of information or perhaps the legacy that you hold from your ancestors). This first step lays within the feminine, since it is She who gives birth. She brings the formless into form by giving birth physically after having created matter out of Her own resources. In human terms, a pregnant woman grows and nurtures a baby inside and from her own body; however, it is not a new creation but a manifestation into the physical of the soul which is a preexisting energy (bringing the formless into form).

Without claiming the below to be a manual of manifestation or the recipe to success, let us break down into fragments what we need, at least in the first stage, in order to manifest.

Be aware that you wish to manifest something. This is hardly the most difficult part; as it happens, I have not met a single person so far that does not want something, and most of the time this wanting also generates some amount of frustration, so it becomes difficult not to be aware of it. When I talk about awareness I am referring to the quality of being conscious of it, which means having in mind, actively remembering, that you are on a mission.

Be clear about what that is. This part requires some amount of introspection. In the very first stage of life, as a baby or a toddler, we cry because we are not able to either identify or express what it is that we need. Unfortunately, this state of being continues all throughout adulthood for many, it is just that the crying stops or better said that it is silenced and buried inside, resulting in continuous frustration, rage and resentment that is occasionally released by outbursts with different pretexts or on different people whenever given the chance.

When I was not more than four or five, I got a very nice chocolate for Christmas, among other things. It was a very special chocolate, like nothing I had tasted before, and I clearly remember holding the bar which had a carriage and two horses drawn on the wrapping. It was a beautiful illustration. For some years afterwards, I kept on wanting and looking for this same chocolate, not knowing what makes it so special but always identifying it with the wrapping. Until one day when I was offered a piece of a coffee chocolate and realized that what I was looking for all along was actually that specific taste, and that the wrapping had no relevance to my quest whatsoever. So wouldn't you rather know what flavor your favorite chocolate is?

To avoid chasing the wrapping instead of the content, I find that a good exercise is to identify the basic emotion that you are experiencing, which is almost always either a lack of something or a fear. When we lack something, we strive to create and fill that space which we perceive as being empty. When we fear something, we try to remove it, which in turn creates another void which wants to be filled. For instance, let us take the case of someone who is unhappy with their job and ends up concluding that they do not feel appreciated by their boss, despite the considerable efforts they put in on a daily basis. So it is a lack of appreciation which they are experiencing. They might be tempted in this case to try to manifest another job or another boss who will appreciate them at their true perceived value. However, the question they should then ask themselves is, *why* do they have a need to be appreciated? Is it because they have been conditioned to please others? Or because they do not value themselves either, so no matter how much validation they receive from others, it will not be enough to fill that void? Or perhaps they are still trying to compensate for a parent which was not appreciative of them as a child? In any case, only by removing the real cause of the problem, which can be a trauma or a self-limiting belief, will they be able to make a considerable change in their life.

When we get to the real cause of our suffering, it often happens that we are able to fill in that gap ourselves and suddenly there is no need to manifest anything (we start feeling appreciation towards ourselves and no longer crave to receive it from others). If we do not identify the real cause, we might end up chasing job after job, without ever finding that place where we are appreciated. I do not deny that there can be circumstances when we are actually being taken for granted, at work or in a personal relationship, and if one finds that this is the case then it is safe to want to manifest something better. And it is also true that people, and especially the feminine aspect of them, thrive in environments where they feel valued, but it does not follow that we should feel hurt if this is not the case. When we are hurt, there is a *need* to manifest, whereas when we are healed there might be a *willingness* or a *preference* to manifest and that gives a much lighter and joyful quality to our life.

Learn to identify and value what it is in you that can constitute a resource. When I was in school, teachers used to tell me that I have a gift for writing. Which was all very well, except that I did not believe it, so I never really took their praises into consideration. I find that this is a trap that many of us are tempted to fall into because of different reasons: sometimes we don't think that we are enough and other times we don't get the same validation from everyone around (and we assume that if some are not impressed or interested in our skills, it must mean that those who are must be in the wrong). So I would like to emphasize on the word *value*.

The general definition of the term *value*, or at least one of them, is *the regard that something is held to deserve; the importance, worth, or usefulness of something*. Feminine energy wants to feel valued in order to accomplish (as opposed to masculine energy that feels valued after accomplishing); it is not the desire, however, which is important here, but the feeling of it, which in turn attracts more of the same. You might imagine that the first people that should appreciate our value are our family and close ones, ahead of anyone else, but what happens if they do not? Presuming that we do have them around, and as well intended as they might be, people might also suffer from their own wounds which prevent them to truly *see* us or express themselves in an appropriate way. So the first person that needs to express this appreciation is our own self; this is a resource we all have and it is not a surrogate for other people's respect or validation to us, but a prerequisite. There is a tendency to confuse self-worth with having an inflated ego, but this is not the case. Someone who is full of themselves will usually feel the need to demonstrate it publicly, and often perceives themselves as superior, while someone who has self-worth will just *know* they are worthy (without lacking humility and without comparing themselves to others).

It is not uncommon that people reach a considerably mature stage of their life before they have identified any resourcefulness within, because nobody has ever pointed it out to them. I hear many friends and acquaintances saying things like:

I don't have any particular skill or talent.

or

I am not particularly good at anything.

But is it really so? Or is it because they only think of very specific technical or artistic abilities, such as drawing, having a mind for quantum physics or being good at sports?

Undoubtedly, modern society favors abilities and qualities pertaining to the masculine aspect of energy because they are displayed in a more obvious way and help us achieve practical goals in life: being assertive, logical, mastering a certain craft, being ambitious and competitive, in other words external displays of power. It is not my intent to minimize their importance in any way, but to point out that by adhering to this principle we end up disregarding and even rejecting our feminine qualities. How many times have you been complimented on being empathic, intuitive, compassionate, caring or going with the flow, which are all expressions of internal power? By denying these aspects of us, we have built a society where masculine energy dominates (a patriarchal society as we call it) and therefore we feel obliged to only develop this side of ourselves. This is also why technical and scientific progress prevail spirituality, manufactured prevails natural, and packaging (the external) prevails content (the internal). It could be argued that there is nothing wrong with this and that it is a consequence of human evolution, but if evolution is only measured with half a cup, then it is not growth, but an imbalance.

By losing the feminine (the internal), we also lose our internal power. How do we know if we have lost it? The inability to attract and to manifest what we want and what is good for us is a lack of internal power. If you felt guided to read this book, then most likely you have lost it and are trying to get it back. The need to be liked and to please is also a loss of personal power (that is not to say that having inner power means being displeasing, inconsiderate or unaccommodating to others; these would classify as something else). An honest self-appraisal will let you know if this is the case.

So, start developing your sense of self-worth and value your feminine aspects as well, in addition to your masculine, because as you might remember from the previous chapter, it is the feminine energy which attracts, and the energy of worth, of acknowledging this resource within, attracts more resource and leads to manifestation. Start appreciating yourself for how you do the small things in life and your soft skills: maintaining your household, connecting to people, enquiring after the sick, being able to look after yourself, making someone laugh etc. Ultimately, your sense of self-worth should not be conditioned by anything, but I find that it is useful to first identify things you like about yourself, since measuring your own value just by existing is a difficult concept to grasp in the beginning and is often misunderstood.

Having established how this first step in manifestation works from the energetic point of view, the second step is the domain of the masculine, the *doer*. I will not go into extensive detail, since it falls out of the scope of this book, but it is necessary to refer to it because the feminine only makes sense in the presence of the masculine. This *doing* mode is sometimes overlooked in the spiritual community since there is a common belief that you need to express a wish, plant a seed, and then let go and the Universe will do the rest. What letting go means is giving up the expectation of when and how it will happen and stop overthinking, in other words trusting or having faith. It does not necessarily mean that you are exempt from making any effort towards the goal. If you want to find a job, you had better start sending out CVs (resumés). If you want to find a partner that has certain qualities to them, ask yourself first if you display the same qualities; if you do not, then it is unlikely that you will find what you expect since like attracts like. So if you wish for your future partner or spouse to be a good communicator, start by being one yourself and perhaps do some reading or attend a workshop on this topic, if necessary.

Sometimes the Universe surprises us and delivers when we least expect it and with no apparent effort, but rest assured that you have done something to attract it, even if it was unconscious or you have forgotten about it. And this holds true for all things and events, regardless of whether they are perceived to be positive or negative (the latter almost always sparks debate because the feeling of being deserving is much more pleasant than that of being imperfect). However, the so-called *bad* experiences do not necessarily come because we have done something *bad* before or because we deserve it, but because we are essentially consciousness that wants to experience, regardless of how this experience might be evaluated in human terms.

There is also another side of the coin: the permanent state of *doing*, without any *being*. Very masculine men, for instance, have a real problem with doing nothing or even holding still. The more masculine energy one expresses, the greater the need for moving and doing. It is one of the reasons why some men become considerably difficult to deal with for family and friends after retirement because they take on unhealthy habits or behaviors; the absence of a daily routine and of a job to invest in, results in a toxic accumulation of energy. This habit of being permanently active without being able to relax is nowadays also seen in women that have been conditioned to be overly masculine in order to cope with everyday life.

In terms of manifestation, the same state of excess masculine energy is capable of great accomplishments, but not necessarily the type that bring peace and fulfillment. Not putting the feminine first, the intuition, the feeling, the introspection, results in making things happen for the sake of it; getting promotions, money, public recognition because it is the general perception of what accomplishments should be, regardless of whether they are what we actually crave for, or not. And most of the time, they are not. In other words, the correct identification of what it is that we really want is missing. This is what often drives people to wonder what the meaning of life is, since despite all they have done and achieved, they still feel empty on the inside.

This brings me to the last (but not least) topic which I feel should be discussed in relation to manifestation, which is the reasoning behind it. A good exercise to have in mind whenever we feel called to create something is asking ourselves why we want that specific thing. The ego always wants to be in the front row, and asks for things which feed it, things which provide attention, validation, praise, appreciation from others. All these are in fact expressions of a single basic state of being, which is love (love has many facets and can take many forms, of different vibrations), and to which we all crave to go back to. When we perceive a lack of love in our life, we seek it in whatever or whoever can provide a glimpse of it, and some of the most horrible human acts throughout history have been done out of this desire to feel loved. So one way to get the ego out of the picture is to love yourself. The notorious phrase *love thy neighbor as thyself* has a very subtle temporality to it: first comes the love for self, which then provides a model for how one should love others. It is not about being selfish, but about learning how to fill our cup so that we don't end up emptying others' or trying to fill it with something that doesn't belong there. More on how to find and keep love in our lives will be discussed in Chapter 7: Spirit. Ultimately, when we are able to connect permanently with the vibration of love, we find that there is not much left to manifest because we already have all that we need.

Although the subject of this chapter is far from having been exhausted here, for the sake of clarity I would like to summarize the main ideas detailed above:

- The feminine principle (feeling, intuiting, being) precedes the masculine principle (doing) in the law of manifestation.
- Self-worth and self-love are a prerequisite for being able to manifest.
- Qualities and attributes falling in the feminine spectrum of energy are just as important to cherish and develop as the masculine ones.
- Being able to remove the ego out of the reasoning for which we seek to manifest acts as a catalyst for our future sense of fulfilment.

Chapter 3

Gratitude

The art of living in the 'now'

For those of you who are part of the spiritual community, living in gratitude might be a notion already discovered and explored, since it is a common belief that life without gratitude defies the purpose of it. Far from authoring an essay on why and how to be grateful, I would like to emphasize on a less obvious aspect of it, which is that it is intimately connected with living in the present moment (which many refer to as mindfulness – although this term has other connotations as well).

Being grateful is all about what you are, do and experience in the present moment, therefore practicing it is a great tool in remaining anchored in the present without allowing yourself to live in the past or in the future, which is so tempting to the human brain. Even when grateful for something that happened in the past, we are still experiencing it in the present, so the connection with the present moment is always there. Never-ending movies and scenarios of what will or could have been, run through our minds, whether we are aware of them or not, to the point that this becomes a natural state of living for us and we end up identifying ourselves with the mind. Humans, just like other forms of life, being multidimensional (with physical, mental, emotional and spiritual dimensions), should not identify themselves with one or two of these bodies and forget all about the others. By denying certain aspects of ourselves, we are prevented from experiencing life to the fullest and therefore remain unfulfilled, always chasing after whatever we perceive happiness to be. It is also advisable to learn how to integrate these dimensions, if we are to understand how life in the Universe works and why it is that we have a physical body (which we could theoretically do without, since we are eternal and formless beings).

When I was a child, time seemed to hold still, the world was full of mysteries and wonders and I could not have imagined a better life, at least most of the time, and I am sure many of you are able to relate to this. It was not because I had all the toys I wanted, or I was never sick or did not experience any sort of lack, but it was because I did not mind it. I was not concerned with what I did not have, but with what I had. The experience of getting a present, regardless of what it was, of playing with other children or of eating a piece of cake, was so exhilarating that I did not feel a need to compare the actual moment with the past, think of what else I would like to have, or compare myself to others. In other words, I was fully in the present moment. This is the natural state of being when we come into physical form because we have not yet forgotten completely why we are here. Forgetting comes in a later stage of life and is what we now incorrectly identify as growing up. In the Bible, it is stated that Jesus said:

Assuredly, I say to you, unless you are converted and become as little children, you will by no means enter the kingdom of heaven.

In other words, until you learn how to live in the present and be fully connected with yourself and with everything that there *is*, you will not be able to experience the greatness of God.

Being present is inherently a feminine quality; feminine energy yearns to be, while the masculine yearns to do. Doing, while undoubtedly essential for growth and evolution, implies that you are missing something or want something better, to go somewhere else, experience something else. Of course, it is necessary to keep moving forward, but it does not follow that stopping and experiencing where you are, by just being, should be disregarded. If you have taken the effort to reach a certain place or goal, do yourself a favor and allow yourself to enjoy it and allow it to fill you up, whatever that is. What we are tempted to do instead is immediately rush to do more or accomplish something else. I hear many nowadays expressing a wish to live a slower life, after being exhausted and overwhelmed by an extremely fast pacing existence. A perfectly valid point of view, as long as we keep in mind that *slowing down* does not necessarily mean having more time to do things, but taking the time to enjoy them. There are people who spend their whole life striving or waiting to reach a specific goal or have a certain life standard, but once they get there, they find themselves unable to enjoy it because they do not know how to just be. So being grateful and being present are inseparable, which is why I say that gratitude is a basic feminine attribute.

One might ask, especially faced with the difficulties of life, what is there to be grateful for? Well, since it is easier to start with the simplest and most obvious things, how about being grateful for your physical body? This is the densest of the bodies and the easiest to perceive and experience. As mentioned before, gratitude starts with being present, being aware, so are you really aware of your body? If not, then it is not surprising that you are not able to be grateful.

By being aware I mean consciously experiencing not only the inside of your body, but also the way it interacts with the environment and the sensations which result out of this interaction.

A first thing to do is start being aware of any tensions in your body. Even if for just five minutes, sit in a comfortable position or lay down and scan your body from top to bottom, having in mind the intention to relax. You will notice, at a closer look, that quite a lot of muscles in your body are contracted most of the time and almost always unnecessarily. When you are sitting on a chair or working in front of the computer, there is no need to have a tense forehead, a clenched jaw or tension in your abdomen for instance. These muscles are neither used for sitting, nor for performing any task you might need to perform while sitting there, whether that is thinking, speaking, typing etc., so why are you maintaining them contracted? It is of course unconscious, you will say, and that is correct; it is what we commonly refer to as stress, and from a subtler perspective it reflects the almost permanent state of being in your masculine energy. Your body is always ready to do, to perform, to react. It is like being in a constant state of threat, which will prompt the body to secrete adrenaline, which in turn creates more tension, so on and so forth.

So, practice relaxing your body as often as you can. You will find that after a while, it becomes natural to quickly identify and relax those tense muscles, and that by bringing softness in your body, you allow yourself to feel more and to be more present. By being in a relaxed state most of the time, you can also further identify how your body reacts to emotions, people and other stimuli. When we are in the presence of an unpleasant or harmful stimulus or even when we think of it, our body responds with tension, so by closing up. We are closing ourselves up from receiving that energy which is not beneficial to us, and that is an essential characteristic of all living creatures, which is the *fight or flight*, or survival mode. This mechanism is not only designed to help us survive, but to also serve us in non-life-threatening situations, such as deciding whether a place, an activity or even a person is beneficial to us. In other words, being present is a wonderful tool in the decision-making process, since we always instinctively know what is good for us and what is not. Pay special attention to the area of the solar plexus since that is where emotions are felt more intensely. This reconciling of your physical and emotional bodies will eventually help in creating a conscious union between the two, which is a solid basis for further integrating the mental and ultimately the energy body. When you are eventually able to observe the way energy moves through the physical body, this will bring you a sense of lightness and joy per se.

Once you manage to be fairly present in your physical body, you find that enjoying what you can perceive with your senses is much easier. The simple act of eating will become more intense because you suddenly notice tastes and textures of food, which used to pass by unnoticed even if you have had that particular food a hundred times before. And that in itself is something you will be grateful for. Spending time out in nature, being with a dear friend or stroking a cat's fur is far more pleasant if you allow yourself to be filled by it, and this is when you come to be grateful for the small things in life.

Being grateful for your physical body also implies appreciating it as a beautiful and unique expression of consciousness, or of the formless becoming form. Living in an age when beauty standards are more than defined, makes it difficult not to compare ourselves with others or with whatever might be considered as beautiful. Explaining to someone, and especially a child, that there is no such thing as a standard definition of what beauty or attractiveness is and that it has become merely a social convention (not much different from the agreed retirement age), is becoming increasingly difficult. Therefore, instead of being grateful for our physical form, we are accustomed since early age to focus on what we are that is *not* considered to be beautiful by the social standard, and furthermore, to try to conceal it or change it. Again, we are in the doing mode and not in the being. Unbelievably, women who make constant efforts to make themselves look more feminine with the help of plastic surgery inevitably end up exhibiting excess masculine energy. Remember that feminine energy does not need to do anything in order to attract, and that attraction is not only based on physical characteristics. This is not equivalent with the statement that plastic surgery should not be attempted or that there is anything wrong in having it, but it is rather a call to question our motive for wanting it and to also know when to stop.

Having established the above, anyone can find things that they like and appreciate in their body, things to be grateful for. Show your body that you appreciate it: if you like your hair, look after it; if you like your nails, keep them nicely manicured. The physical body, even in its state of high density, is still energy, and will react to your feelings and emotions towards it. When you are grateful for it, it will also feel better. Last but not least, be grateful for your state of health, even if not perfect.

The emotional body is much subtler and more difficult to master, because our emotions are often overlooked when we are engaged in all-consuming activities, and we might even confuse them with thoughts. Of course, emotions will give rise to thoughts of all kinds and vice versa, but it is important to tell one from another. A simple thought is just a piece of information that your brain is processing in a specific moment, whereas emotions are ways we react to our external environment. For instance, let us say that you become uncomfortable at the thought that someone might be late for an appointment with you, because they very often are. As the meeting moment approaches, you become increasingly anxious and the brain starts making up scenarios of how and why this is happening. However, they do show up in time after all. You might be tempted to say to them:

I *thought* that you would be late.

Which you did, but this thought was merely a result of the emotion called 'anxiety'; no actual information was received that they might be late, so there was no information to process, no logical thinking, but an emotion. This is an example of how sometimes overthinking replaces the processing of emotions. If instead you would have stopped and realized that you are just experiencing an episode of anxiety, there would have been no need for the brain to start analyzing, and very possibly your anxiety would have stopped or diminished instead of escalating. You would have perhaps also been grateful for sitting in the sun while waiting, or hearing a bird sing, which you would have most likely not noticed because you were so caught up in your own scenarios.

The emotional body is given to us to experience a wide range of human emotions, not to be used as a means for further confusion. Being aware of your emotions, of how you feel, prevents the brain from going into unnecessary torment and helps to live in the present moment. Feminine energy feels, in other words it is aware through feeling, and is able to identify it as just feeling and nothing else. Being emotional is normal and there is no need to judge oneself for it, but also no need to let our emotions hijack our intellect. So a practical way of being aware of the emotional body is by becoming accustomed to the statement *I feel* [...] (then identify the specific emotion), whether it is said out loud or not (and undoubtedly women do say it out loud much more than men). You will notice that almost instantly, the mental chatter stops. By making it a habit to state what exactly you are feeling you not only identify feelings which otherwise might go unnoticed, but you are also able to get to know yourself better; you might conclude that you feel angry or resentful, or on the contrary happy, much more often than you thought. Communicating and connecting with yourself is just as important as doing it with others. When one takes ownership of their inner world, one feels much more aware of the outer because less energy is wasted in processing thoughts which are ultimately of no consequence. And until ownership of the emotional body is achieved, being present and being grateful are both considerably difficult.

A natural conclusion of the above is that the mental body, which is the sum of all processes which serve us in making logical deductions, organizing information, problem solving, taking decisions and where our memories are stored, is far less active than we think, and this is because what we perceive as being *mental* is actually just the emotional body gone rogue. Unlike the previously described body, this one is masculine in nature, and by definition, the realm of the intellect. By being able to make a distinction between the two, and by being aware of the dynamics between them, one integrates their feminine and masculine aspects. I call this process reconciling the brain with the heart, although not in actual terms, of course. If you find yourself in a situation where the brain and the heart are pulling you in opposite directions from the point of view of decision making, then these aspects of you are not yet reconciled. They are there to complete, and not antagonize one another. Since all life forms are built to function in a coherent way (which means that all the sub-parts are in harmony), there is no reason to believe that humans should function any differently just because we might perceive ourselves as more complex.

As a practical example, you have been offered a job and are trying to decide whether you should take it or not. Theoretically, it seems to be a very good opportunity and there is no obvious reason why you should refuse it. But your gut instinct is telling you that something is not right. Will you follow your intellect (the masculine) or your feelings (the feminine)? Well, the answer is you should follow neither, but try to reconcile them. The problem here is that you are perceiving yourself as duality, whereas in reality you are just overlapping the two aspects of yourself. Once you can identify the exact emotion you are experiencing and why, things will become much clearer. In this particular example, if what you are experiencing is, for instance, a feeling of insecurity towards the future, ask yourself first if you would ever be able to feel secure about it. The answer is obviously no; there is no way one can tell what will happen in the future, so this emotion of yours is not a good basis for decision making. So it would be preferable that you follow your intellect, if it is telling you that this job prospect is able to fulfill certain needs you have (other than that of controlling the future). If, on the other hand, you experience a feeling of not being safe in that specific professional environment (to express your authenticity, to be yourself, to rely on others or whatever else it takes for you to feel safe), then bear in mind that changing that environment will most likely be impossible, so it is safe to honor your feelings and look for another job instead.

Again, we see that the feminine comes before the masculine, the awareness of the emotional body precedes the decision making by the mental body. At the same time the logical thinking can, up to a certain extent, be applied to clarify the feeling, in other words the two aspects can be reconciled.

To go back on the concept of gratitude, you might wonder how this discussion on the emotional and mental bodies is connected to it. It is safe to state that gratitude comes from what we have or perceive to have in the present. The perception and the awareness that we have inside of us all the resources to be able to live a coherent life without being confused and without the drama of decision making, leads to gratitude for just being. So there are numerous things to be grateful for and it is not even necessary to look for them outside, but rather look to know oneself.

To summarize, here is the takeaway massage on gratitude:

- Being grateful is a result of being present and fully connected to ourselves.
- We are comprised of physical, emotional, mental and spiritual bodies, and the awareness of each of them leads to a better knowing of oneself and to the ability to stay present.
- The emotional body is feminine, while the mental body is masculine; the balance of the two leads to a cohesive existence.

- Connecting with our feminine aspect by becoming aware of our feelings precedes the connection with our masculine which reasons and takes decisions.

Chapter 4

Beauty

Consciousness revealing itself

According to the standard definition, beauty is represented by the qualities in a person or an object which give pleasure to the senses or to the mind. I find this to be an incomplete and inaccurate definition, which is not surprising since it is such a complex and relative term. What appeals to the senses could be quite different things to different people, not to mention that some people have a higher capacity to *sense*, which makes them more likely to notice and appreciate beauty. So we could argue that beauty is not an actual concept or term describing the person or object being contemplated, but an experience of the one who contemplates. It is therefore a perception or a state of awareness; as we say,

Beauty is in the eyes of the beholder.

We could even say that beauty itself does not exist, but only the perception of it.

Why is it that beauty is considered the domain of the feminine and not of the masculine? One could say that both are equally interested in it, which is correct. The difference is that while the masculine is inclined to contemplate it, the feminine is more inclined to create it. Whether they are creating it in themselves or in the external environment, it represents the capacity of the feminine to be aware, or to be conscious of the potential that is there. Putting makeup on, creating a piece of clothing, looking after a garden are all examples of how the feminine uses the potential of what is already there, in order to create more awareness. Everything is already there, but by making it more beautiful, one enhances the experience of it. If you often walk through a building or a space which is unaesthetically organized, you probably do not even look around, or if you do happen to observe something, it would probably be the most unpleasant features which may stand out. If one day you walk inside again, but after someone has redecorated or reorganized the space in an appropriate way, not only do you make note of it and appreciate it, but you might also observe aspects which have gone unnoticed previously. You might, for instance, suddenly become aware of how sunny the building is, or notice the beautiful view from the windows. The sun and the view have always been there, but you were probably not aware or conscious of them. Suddenly, you *see* the environment and you like it. And it is because someone else has seen the potential of it beyond appearances and taken the trouble to show it to you as well.

So your capacity of *seeing* and revealing beauty around, even if not obvious, is a measure of your feminine energy. A sign that you are not in tune with the feminine aspect of yourself is not being able to find beauty around you. If you are on a bus or on the street and you often find yourself thinking that people around are ugly, you have certainly lost touch with it. Just as beauty cannot be defined, ugliness cannot either, so what you see is just your perception. This does not mean that you are expected to find everyone attractive, but you can identify beauty everywhere if you wish to (not by putting your rose-tinted glasses on, but by increasing your awareness, by seeing them as they truly are). For example, men with excess masculine energy have difficulties in connecting to partners beyond the generally accepted standards of beauty; their choice of partners will be mostly based on obvious physical attributes which make a woman attractive from the point of view of general beauty standards. Women who are disconnected from their feminine are not interested in any type of manifestation of beauty, whether it is in nature, art, a person, or object, or even in themselves.

What is concerning is that the perception of beauty is limited to beliefs on how exactly another person should look, and never focuses on our own inner thoughts and processes, and as I mentioned before, beauty in itself is more of an experience than an attribute per se. So, if you want to become more in tune with beauty as a feminine aspect of yours, see it and experience it more, start working from inside out.

First of all, analyze how you find yourself in terms of beauty. Do you generally like yourself, or do you only like some of your traits, or none at all? I am not only referring to physical attributes, but it is good to start with them since they are more obvious, then move on to subtler traits. Once you identify something you like, make a habit in reminding yourself of it on a regular basis, perhaps write it down in a notebook, or why not on the bathroom mirror. Sometimes we discover things we never thought of before, in other words we are not aware of our own beauty. You can also ask a close friend to tell you what they find beautiful in you, provided you have an honest and caring relationship with them. You might be surprised by what you find out. On the other side, identify what it is that you do *not* like about yourself and why. Is it because you are comparing yourself to others, or because someone else has once been offensive about it? If this is the case, then they are not appropriate reasons because they have nothing to do with your own person. You cannot measure yourself with someone else's cup, just like you cannot dislike a certain food just because someone else does. And I find that most of the time, this is what happens; if you are able to be reasonably objective, you will also come to the conclusion that it is difficult to find reasons for not liking yourself that have nothing to do with other people's standards.

Another method to reevaluate the way you see yourself and

the concept of beauty is taking a closer look at your wardrobe. Does it suit your personality? Do the pieces make you feel good when you wear them? It is not about how many clothes you have or if they are fashionable or not, but about them suiting your figure and your personality. Having bought a piece of clothing because it looks good on the mannequin or because it is trendy but it does not complement your body type, will not help in making you feel more attractive; on the contrary. The fabrics are also of consequence here. It is common that most clothes nowadays are made of synthetic materials, some of better quality than others. If something does not feel right or is uncomfortable because it is rigid, has a plastic feel to it, or is too tight, don't wear it. Forcing yourself to do things or fit into them in order to be appealing to others is not feminine, contrary to the common belief. The feminine likes softness and comfort, so choose pleasant and soft fabrics. If you can afford silk wear it, if not find something else that you enjoy the feeling of. Same goes for men, who would benefit from wearing more natural fibers, even though it might not always be possible. If your work requires that you wear a suit, compensate by what you wear in your spare time.

Secondly, finding and keeping beauty in your life is also about creating a pleasant environment to live in. Seemingly insignificant things can have a great impact on the way you feel when you are at home, so think about what entices your senses. This could be a comfortable sofa or mattress, having plants and flowers around the house, relaxing music playing in the background, scented candles etc... The price of an object is not directly proportional with its aesthetic potential, so you do not need to make big investments to appreciate your environment as being pleasant to the senses. Being comfortable in your own space when you finish work or school helps you appreciate the small things in life; if you find that you have the tendency to avoid being at home, one of the reasons could be that the space is not adequate for you, even if not always obvious. Maybe decluttering it or adding some more color would make you appreciate it more, so take some time to discover what works for you.

Food, or better said its presentation, can also be aesthetic (or not). We are accustomed to think that only on special occasions should we make the effort to serve meals in a pleasant way, such as in beautiful dishes or on a nice tablecloth. Some barely take any time to cook a proper meal for themselves, let alone put it together in an appealing way. I once saw a family coming from a low-income background winning millions in the lottery and buying an exquisite, large house in a select neighborhood, after which they kept eating from plastic crockery, since this is what they were accustomed to. I am not criticizing the simple lifestyle, nor their background, but only pointing out that we might have the tendency of unnecessarily depriving ourselves of beauty in our lives. It is not necessary to go out of your way on a daily basis to deliver a nicely put-together dinner, but consider doing so from time to time, in accordance with your own means. In some areas of the world, food was traditionally served (and still is) on banana leaves for several reasons, one of them being because they are a cheap resource. Nevertheless, they are certainly much more aesthetic to eat from than plastic dishes, and healthier.

Opening ourselves slowly to the small things in life which reflect beauty is relaxing, nurturing and leads to attracting more beauty, if we allow it to. One of the reasons we might not allow it is low self-esteem; we do not consider ourselves worthy of beauty. Those falling into this category usually do not find beauty in themselves either, and this belief is difficult to remove because oftentimes it is linked to trauma and old wounds. Lack of self-esteem is acquired, and not something we are born with, therefore it is also possible to overcome it, provided one becomes aware of it. This is a complex issue which I will not debate in detail here, but one sign that you might suffer from low self-esteem is resistance to beauty. Do you often catch yourself compromising and buying the cheaper and lower quality version of items you need, even if you are perfectly able to afford them from the financial point of view? Are you reluctant to wearing your nicer clothes because you feel that it is usually unnecessary to dress up? Do you find yourself judging people who spend more money and energy on such things? Although moderation and intelligent use of resources are virtues and also help protect the environment, in most cases these might be signs that you do not hold yourself in high esteem. It is worth giving it a good thought as uncomfortable as it may be. Letting go of such self-limiting beliefs is extremely cathartic and will have a beneficial impact on all areas of your life.

As to the energetics of aesthetics, I would like to explain the impact beauty has on the energetic body. Since we have already established that beauty is an inside job, imagine what would happen if this was completely missing in ourselves. The inability to enhance your experiences by finding the good, the pleasant and ultimately the perfection of nature leads to living a low-profile life, like an engine always working on the lowest level. This creates stagnation in the energy field since you are not using it at its fullest capacity. The energy body is composed of different vibrations, much like a musical instrument able to produce different notes. If certain chords of the instrument remain unused, they eventually become dysfunctional or decay. It is the chords of our souls able to produce the highest vibration that are also reacting to beauty, which explains why we might not feel the need to use them on a regular basis (they are not essential to our existence here). One is perfectly able to go through life in the physical form completely ignoring the use of beauty because it is not practical, but if you have ever met such a person, you probably found them difficult to be around in the long term. Only being interested in the immediate and most basic needs makes us heavy from the energetic point of view. In terms of polar energies, the masculine being mostly concerned with the practical aspects of life, it is not surprising that it is not overly concerned by beauty and does not feel the urge to create more of it. The feminine, on the other side, resides more in the top notes of the instrument, so it connects naturally to the subtler and more ethereal domains, which explains why people with strong feminine energy take a keen interest in spirituality, art, nature, and all other things that upgrade one's existence.

So I hope this provides a better understanding of why beauty is so closely connected to feminine energy and how to express it more in your daily life, and would like to point out the basic ideas discussed here:

- Beauty is not an attribute of an object nor of a person being contemplated, but an experience of the one contemplating.
- Feminine energy is able to create, perceive and reveal beauty, even when it is not obvious.
- Connecting to beauty in everyday life by creating a pleasant experience for yourself with the help of small, ordinary things like objects, clothing and food, helps enhance the feminine aspect.
- Lack of self-esteem can create resistance to beauty in oneself and around.
- Being able to see and appreciate beauty helps the energy body reach a high vibrational state.

Chapter 5

Flow

The power to let go

To go with the flow is a very commonly used phrase, meaning moving along with something or someone else without restrictions, in practical terms not having a specific agenda and reacting spontaneously to events and people. But let us dive deeper into the symbolic meaning of it and find how it is connected to feminine energy.

In physics, *flow* is defined as the quantity of fluid that passes a point per unit time; in other contexts, it can also mean moving in a continuous or steady stream. Without going into the science of it, I would firstly like to point out that it refers to fluids or other things which, to a certain extent, have qualities that can be assimilated to those of fluids. In the Zen tradition it is believed that the Universe is made up of five elements: water, fire, metal, wood and earth, and the water element (considered to be of feminine in nature) is the only one that the principle of flowing can be applied to. Flowing is something that water (the feminine) does on its own, it is its primary nature and does not need external input to do so. On the contrary, it is more difficult to contain it than to let it flow (keeping water in a vessel or in a dam is only possible if no cracks are present, and as soon as a minor fissure occurs, it is only a matter of time until water finds its way out, and very often it does so in a violent way). So feminine energy needs to flow by definition; when contained, even if calm on the surface, it holds immense power and should be treated carefully.

Living in such a structured and restrictive world as the present one, does not easily allow us to flow. Most of our days are scheduled from dusk to dawn; we speak, do, wear and eat what we have been taught is appropriate, so much that we have largely become unaware of it. Being restricted is, in a manner of speech, our second nature. I do not deny that some structure and education are necessary in any civilized society, but one must be aware of the tendency to live as such permanently. This structure giving the sense of protection and control, it is not surprising that we have become so comfortable with it that living outside of this order of things, even for a very short period of time, is often perceived as unsafe and makes us uneasy. We are living in a masculine world, as also stated in previous chapters, so the feminine is either completely suppressed in the process, or on the contrary, yearns to frustration to be set free, and when it does finally manage to escape, it is almost invariably destructive on its way out. This is what having a nervous breakdown or a burnout actually is; since the emotional body represents the feminine aspect of us, such physiological and psychological events are a mere manifestation of feminine energy trying to escape restrictions.

So we must learn how to flow, if we want to maintain a balanced life, and this applies to the physical, the emotional and the energetic bodies, and I will describe all three aspects here. They are not separate from each other, but interconnected, which means that stagnation of the flow in one of the bodies can lead to the others being blocked as well.

Emotional flow

The more feminine energy one holds, the more they should allow themselves to flow because stagnant energy becomes toxic, and signs of feminine toxicity are for example excessive or inappropriate outbursts of emotions, being constantly annoyed and edgy, or being passive-aggressive (while all these can be normal ways of expressing anger of frustration, overdoing it and manifesting them in a hurtful or violent way towards other people falls in the spectrum of emotional toxicity). So if you feel that you are constantly on the edge of snapping or shouting at others, it is advisable to stop and evaluate whether there is a lack of flow in any area of your life. Perhaps you feel that you don't have enough freedom of expression, your schedule is too busy and you don't get enough downtime, or there is too much routine in your life.

The opposite of being able to flow is being rigid, and here I would like to emphasize on the difference between rigidity and discipline. For instance, if you have a certain weight or fitness goal in mind and can get yourself out of the house to work out at the gym despite the fact that you are not in the mood or the weather is bad, this is a sign of discipline. If, on the other hand, you always go out of your way to accommodate it in your schedule or expect others to accommodate it in theirs, or you generally work out despite the fact that you are unwell or sick, this is a sign of being rigid. In other words, not being allowing and accommodating towards other activities and people in your life just because you have it in your mind that you *must* do something, even with negative consequences, is a lack of flow. Having a need for strict planning and being frustrated if something disturbs it, or feeling uncomfortable in its absence, is a sign that you are no longer able to flow. I can vouch from my own experience how difficult it is to tell discipline from rigidity, since I had suffered from the latter for most of my childhood and early adult life. An exercise that helped me when I was trying to overcome it was asking myself, whenever something unexpected or unplanned came up, if this event was beneficial for me or not. If a good friend calls interrupting your usual Saturday routine, asking if you would like to do something fun together that day, something you enjoy, do yourself a favor and take the opportunity to do so, even if it was not scheduled and could ruin your cleaning or workout plans. Another exercise is to ask yourself if this routine of yours is beneficial itself in that specific moment; if you are in the habit of doing house cleaning every Saturday (a healthy habit most of the time), perhaps it would not be beneficial to do it if you feel very tired or unwell, in which case it is safe to skip it and look after yourself. And last but not least, try to do something new or do usual things differently, on a regular basis In other words, try to be more spontaneous.

Physical flow

Physical flow, as expected, refers to movement. It is necessary to get a certain amount of physical exercise on a daily basis, but it is important to keep in mind that this amount can be quite variable between individuals, depending on their energy profile, body type, gender, age and occupation, and perhaps other factors as well, such as health and the climate they live in. It is popular to follow influencers that we find inspiring in terms of physical health and fitness, to get personal trainers or enroll in fitness programs, but I find that before doing so, we should get in touch with ourselves and find out what exactly we need rather than want. While some of these training programs are tailored to the individual up to a certain extent, there are a few aspects which are overlooked, so I feel guided to point them out.

First of all, the type of movement beneficial to you depends on where you are on the masculine-feminine spectrum. The more masculine energy one expresses, the more active and strenuous forms of movement they will require. Masculine energy is not about flow, but being pointed outwards; it is natural that it wants to get out, and it should, because overaccumulation can potentially result in destructive behavior and even violence. The more feminine energy one holds, the more flowing, light movement they will require, such as dancing, stretching, yoga or Pilates, and sometimes, although it may seem counterintuitive, it is good not to move at all. You will probably ask how not moving is beneficial, but stillness is actually an active principle and not a passive one, in the sense that it allows a state of relaxation following a more intense activity and this in itself is a flow. So, alternating tension and relaxation is a flow, and both need each other in order for the system to thrive and keep moving forward. Therefore, too much strenuous exercise in a woman who holds a lot of feminine energy can actually block this flow and sometimes this blockage becomes physically obvious in the form of headaches or muscle knots. If you experience this after high impact forms of exercise, perhaps you could consider trying something gentler and see how your body reacts.

Secondly, integrating fitness within the concept of flow means that you should strive to respect your body as much as possible, and not cross its boundaries. The body is always talking to us, but we do not really stop to listen because we are not accustomed to paying any attention. Every day, our body is bombarded with physical, chemical and biological information and makes considerable efforts to process it, while still maintaining its balance. Every day, our immune system fights thousands of foreign microorganisms, molecules and tumor cells which we do not even come to be aware of because they are cleared from our system before producing any pathological signs. Sometimes in this process, we might feel inexplicably tired, we might not be able to sleep properly, or wake up with the feeling of not being 100% well. It is a sign that the body is doing something in order to recover its balance, its yin-yang flow, so it is important to respect it. This might mean adapting our fitness activities to something like taking a walk or doing a light stretch, instead of swallowing two tablets of ibuprofen and heading out for a cardio session.

I was once trying to find a clear definition of what the concept of health and fitness is, for me personally. I do not think I have found a very complete and comprehensive one, but I do know what health and fitness are *not*. They are not: looking and feeling identical every day and over the whole life span, or never having any discomfort, aches or illness symptoms. If you have a cold, or a headache, that is all right; it doesn't necessarily mean that you are not healthy, it is just your body trying to maintain its flow, so allow it by giving it more rest and proper food. Of course, concerning any recurrent symptoms of any kind, these will need medical attention. As the yin-yang diagram suggests, nothing is ever perfect or complete: there is always some yin in the yang and vice versa. Even in the utmost state of health, there can be potential for disease and in the ultimate state of disease there is potential for healing. The same is applicable to weight fluctuations; most people probably have at least a 5% to 10% change in body weight throughout their lives and it is a natural consequence of fluctuation in hormones, changes of routine or lifestyle and even location (if it involves moving to a different country or climate area). Do not punish your body by trying to make it fit in a certain pair of jeans, when all it might need is some time to adapt. Remember that your body has its own intelligence (since it is just a physical manifestation of consciousness), and it also feels rejection and judgement, and will not react in a positive way.

Physical signs of impaired flow of energy are very stiff joints and ligaments and tensions in certain areas of your body, especially the neck, shoulders and solar plexus, and also excessive weight gain (although I should mention that if you have gained too much weight, there could also be other causes in addition to the absence of flow). These physical signs can be caused by lack of proper movement, but they can also be a sign of stagnation in the energy body, since the physical body is just a denser form of energy, as it was stated before.

Energetic flow

The energetic body is intimately overlapped on the physical one. It lays inside the physical, but also stretches outside, and is composed of different layers, the external ones creating some amount of friction with the physical aspect; when one becomes aware of the energetic body, that friction can be felt especially on the most sensitive areas of the skin, such as the palms. The issue of how energy moves inside the body is overly complex and I will not go into detail, but I will just refer to a few simple and more practical ideas.

Being much lighter than matter, the energetic body is more sensitive to movement and flows easier, just like less viscous fluids flow easier than the denser ones. In a manner of speech, it is fluid itself. Therefore, whenever we move our bodies it moves with us, but it also does so in less obvious circumstances like for instance when biking or riding a horse, standing in the wind or in a body of flowing water. This is because air and water as primary elements interact very easily with energy (they are its primordial physical manifestations). Breathing not only affects the physical, but also the energetic aspect. When we breathe in and the diaphragm contracts, the energetic body contracts as well and the outer layers come closer to our physical core. When we breathe out, it expands. So breathing properly and in a conscious way is important for the flow of energy.

Spending time out in nature is essential for our energetic well-being, and consequently, the modern and urban lifestyle of indoor living which most of us are accustomed to leads to stagnation of this energy, and so does excessive exposure to cold temperatures and improper diet (especially overconsumption of meat, refined sugars and dairy).

So what are the consequences of a lack of flow in the energetic body? At the very least, it causes a low drive, tiredness, negative emotions and depression, but in more severe cases it causes physical ailments. Illness can be, to a certain extent, a result of our energy body experiencing blockages. The epitome of energetic blockages are nodules and tumors, since local accumulation of energy leads to accumulation of matter. Consequently, if we want real healing for our physical bodies we should start with energy work, regardless of whether we are also receiving standard medical care or not. This is a very foreign concept in nowadays society and is considered a controversial topic reserved for yogis and New Age followers, but I find that it is preferable to first experience things before deciding that it is not convincing or suitable for you. Working with a certified Reiki practitioner is an effective way to start, if you are interested in trying energy healing.

Flow in relationships

The dynamics of relationships, regardless of what type they might be, are not much different from the yin-yang principle of inner balance. We have already spoken about the masculine-feminine polarity in the first chapter, so I would just like to point out that the more feminine partner goes with the flow of the masculine one, rather than the other way around. If you are the feminine aspect of a relationship and want to define the polarity better, start by going more with the flow and give up having control, at least over some things.

I would now like to discuss how to maintain the flow and balance of relationships (which we should attempt to achieve, provided we want them to last).

Relationships are constantly evolving and changing, just like we are. Even if ever so slightly, they adapt over time to input from both individuals maintaining this relationship. It is perfectly normal to go through phases when we feel closer and more connected to a person, and phases when we might not have the need or the chance to connect that much, or perhaps at all. I find that oftentimes we are asking too much of our relationships, holding them to a certain standard that we might not be able to reach or maintain permanently. If we have not been in contact with a good friend for a couple of years, we almost invariably reach the conclusion that we have drifted apart, which we may have, but it does not follow that this process cannot be reversed.

So allow your relationship to flow. Two people come in each other's lives when one or both need it, and there might be times when there isn't any such need, so their relationship stops being a priority for a while, or sometimes it ceases permanently to exist. Both scenarios are natural, and one should not reach the conclusion that if a relationship of any kind ended, then it must be that it was a failure, and become bitter over it.

Worthy of note would be that although the physical interaction between two persons might stop, the subtler, energetic connection will always be there if we want it to, and this also holds true if someone passed away. Since we all have energy bodies and energy does not know time and space, people are always interacting on an energetic level, although most are unaware of this. There is always a flow of energy and information, especially between people with a strong and significant connection, such as parent-child or between spouses, siblings and very good friends. Oftentimes, this exchange starts before we physically meet someone and can persist beyond any chance of physical encounter. Some people are more gifted than others in perceiving these energetic connections, but even if this is not the case for you, keep in mind that your thoughts and attitudes towards someone influence the dynamics between the two of you, even if they are not present physically.

As to expectations for romantic partnerships, it is obvious that we live in a world which expects a good and healthy partnership or marriage (and sometimes any marriage, in fact) to last forever. While it is perfectly normal to want this *forever* to be part of our lives, starting any relationship with the firm belief that we will or must get it puts an immense pressure on the relationship and consequently on both partners. More often than we like to admit, at least one of the partners proves themselves less perfect than initially expected, to say at the very least, so be careful what you wish for. And sometimes, just by being in the energy of allowing the possibility that this forever might not happen, lifts up a great amount of stress and makes the relationship lighter and more joyful. So hope for it if you like, but also allow the flow and do not become rigid about it.

In conclusion to the complex topic of this chapter, hardly exhausted here, the below ideas are a good take-home message:

- The capacity to flow is an intrinsic attribute of feminine energy and is essential for a healthy expression of it.
- Excessive structure, routine and control in our life are damaging to the feminine.
- The physical, the emotional and the energetic body are all in need of flow and we can ensure it by proper physical movement and lifestyle, but also by being allowing of ourselves and of others.
- The lack of flow in one of the bodies can determine stagnation in the other bodies as well, and illness can be a consequence of it.
- Interpersonal relationships of all kinds are dynamic and can be nurtured by allowing them to flow and evolve naturally, rather than trying to control their outcome.

Chapter 6

Joy

Life celebrating itself

Joy is an essential need in our lives, and while we may not be immediately aware of this, it becomes obvious when we lose it. Just like the ability to be present in the moment, discussed in Chapter 3, joy is an inherent attribute of any being coming into existence. Youngsters of most evolved species (especially mammals) tend to display a cheerful and playful attitude with no particular reason either than simply existing, and the more evolved they are (or more aware of themselves), the more joyful they seem to be: they play with their siblings, make funny noises, jump and roll over and seem to enjoy everything around. Offspring of underdeveloped species, not so much. So, it goes without saying that humans, being the most aware and evolved on the biological scale, should display at least the same level of joyfulness, even if not necessarily expressed in a similar manner. This is why laughter, the utmost expression of joy, is an exclusive human ability.

But is this behavior so apparent in humans? Perhaps at an early age, but not necessarily afterwards. So, I would like to discuss why we humans have the tendency to lose this state of joy. It is generally believed, and almost accepted as universal truth, that children are joyful due to their innocence and that once faced with the sorrows of life, it is natural that one loses this attribute. But I am not sure this is completely correct. It is not that much about lacking a reason for being joyful, as it is about losing the ability to express it. Yes, as adults we might have less enjoyable tasks to perform, more responsibility and more seemingly negative experiences, but we are also so used to living in this state, that when we do have a reason to be happy, we sometimes overlook it or dismiss the opportunity to express any joy, because we perceive it as transitory and unimportant. So not being joyful is, above all, a habit, and only secondly a natural consequence of life experience. The fact that you've had it rough does not mean that there is no opportunity for joy to come into your life; these two concepts are not interdependent, so it is advisable to treat them as separate.

This habit of not expressing joy, being mostly triggered by increased responsibility, being busy or being on an important mission, is therefore a consequence of living permanently in your masculine energy, the *doer*. Not having reached a goal, not having met a certain need, is more important than being joyful; joy will not pay the bills and will not bring something or someone we lost back, so what is the point of it? If you find yourself validating this logic, then you are favoring your masculine energy over your feminine. The feminine, on the other hand, is all about enjoying (en-*joy*-ing), so not only appreciating what you do have and experience, but also expressing it. Women and generally people holding a lot of feminine energy tend to laugh more and aloud. How often do you laugh? If you cannot remember exactly, then the answer is probably: not too often. I myself was very surprised a while ago, when I realized that despite the fact that I had a generally happy life, I was not laughing any more, almost at all. And consequently, I realized how much I was missing it. So forgetting to be joyful is like I said, mostly just a habit, and having said that, any habit can be reinstalled. You can look for opportunities and people that spark your amusement and allow yourself to laugh out loud unless the time or place are inappropriate. A well-mannered joke is usually safe and can be appreciated even in a professional setting sometimes, although reading the room before saying something or laughing is always advisable. Books and movies can also be a source of good humor, so find out for yourself or remember what works for you after a long day or week at work.

Another behavior that distinguishes humans from other animals, besides laughter, is that of celebrating. To celebrate, among other things, means to honor (an occasion, such as a holiday) especially by solemn ceremonies or by refraining from ordinary business, but also to acknowledge a significant happy event. The tendency to celebrate is also an inborn trait in humans, since there is historical and archeological evidence that ceremonies and rites of passage have been with us since the dawn of civilization. There is evidence, dating up to approximately 40,000 years ago, that we have been celebrating and rejoicing in various aspects of life pretty much since ever. We expressed joy for the fertility of the land and of the humans, for the passing of the seasons, for certain astrological events, in certain cultures even for death. Old times were times when the feminine was worshiped, in certain ages even more than the masculine, and the act of performing a ceremony or a ritual is feminine per se, so it is not surprising that customs, traditions and religious practices involving rituals have lost most of their value and significance in this modern and patriarchal society. But with these, we have also given up joy almost altogether. Just as it is true that behaviors are expressions of states of being, or of archetypes, in other words of energy, it is also true that refraining from certain behaviors suppresses in turn that specific energy.

If you do not resonate with traditions and religion, but still want to reconnect with your feminine, start by defining small rituals for yourself, to celebrate whatever is significant to you or to mark an end (or beginning), even if it is that of a project or just of the week. The ritual can be anything that brings you joy, like having a food you like, buying flowers for yourself, gathering with friends, but also something more ad litteram, such as burning incense and prayer or meditation. By performing these, you are acknowledging something which has been achieved and you are expressing joy for it.

I know that the habit of going out or meeting up with friends is particularly important to many, and it does also count as celebration to a certain extent, but I would like to point out that every celebration which becomes a standard loses its value and oftentimes ends up being taken for granted. It is not uncommon for people with a very active social life to still feel that they lack true joy, and it is because this ritual of gathering has become a way of living. In the old days, both religious and pagan celebrations were held at very precise times of the year and had special significance; they were intercalated into routine work and agricultural activities, fasting and other soberer aspects of everyday life. So there was a healthy alternation between the masculine and the feminine. As a rule, when something becomes regular it stops being special. To many, Christmas has lost its magic not only due to the loss of its religious significance, but also because we are buying and eating excessively throughout the year so there is nothing special left to be done. That is not to say that taking joy in things on a daily basis is wrong, on the contrary, but it is more fulfilling in the long term to keep your expression of joy in proportion to the significance of the event. If you throw a massive party every month, you will feel obliged to do even more on your birthday and probably be unfulfilled because that dose of monthly joy cannot be surpassed, so your birthday does not seem significant any longer.

From the energetic perspective, joy is not an attitude, but a vibration. When you are in a specific vibration, you attract more of it, and this does not mean that you would necessarily have more reasons to be joyful, but you are able to maintain this state of being beyond what is happening around you. Being joyful within despite the circumstances does not equal being insensitive, and you are surely not required to suffer just because some people around do. And here I feel guided to emphasize on the energetic dynamics between people. Joy having a high vibration, partly makes us attract similar people, but also the opposite sometimes occurs (people who lack joy in their lives have the tendency to excessively complain, especially to those that seem more fulfilled). They are the so-called *energy vampires*; consciously, they rely on people who seem happy because they perceive them as stronger and able to provide emotional support, and unconsciously they feed on their energy. Beware of friends or even family members who drain your energy by constantly confiding in you, sharing their misfortunes, or asking for your advice. There is a difference between someone who needs emotional support and someone being toxic, which is that the latter is always doing so, not being able to connect in a different way or provide support back, never following any advice they are given and becoming resentful when you are unavailable or try to set boundaries. You will find that after interacting with them, your own levels of joy seem to have diminished considerably or you might even feel guilty for not being equally unfortunate. One way of assessing the level of health in a relationship of any kind is to determine if the other person supports you in being joyful, because only in the absence of a second agenda and of feelings of envy and resentment, can one do this. If, on the other hand, someone makes you feel guilty or feel obliged to lower your spirit, if they become aggressive, or on the contrary cut you off when you are happy, this is a sign that the relationship is toxic. It is advisable to stop feeding their victim mentality or even minimize contact with them if necessary; as tempting as it might be to help them out of their misery, it is exceedingly difficult to do so unless they are also willing to help themselves. Out of all the vibrational states, authentic joy is the one that attracts darkness the most because it is perceived as a threat to the ego. Joy for just being implies that there is no need for something external, and this state of empowerment is rarely left unattended by darker forces.

Having mentioned the term *authentic joy*, I would also like to define it. As I said, being truly joyful is not an attitude, but a vibration; it is something that comes from within and does not have a need to be necessarily displayed. Consequently, you can easily identify people who have not yet reached this authenticity, because they are displaying joy only outwardly, in a loud and sometimes almost aggressive way. People who are suspiciously energetic, competitive, and have a need to draw attention to themselves by being loud and obviously cheerful all the time, unfortunately, have severe trauma which they are trying to mask. I find that it is these people who need more compassion than anyone, since their wounds go so deep that they have constructed this front for themselves in the attempt to cover them up. So in a way, they manufacture positivity. They also tend to display this behavior permanently, which is unnatural since having certain mood fluctuations (even if not necessarily in a negative sense) is a healthy way of reacting and adapting to everyday life and of coping with our inner universe.

So authentic joy will always be expressed in a moderate and subtle way, and you will find that people experiencing it exude it just by being and not necessarily doing something. They are perceived as good to be around and have a positive impact on others, as opposed to someone just displaying a front, who will become tiring after a while. Joy being an aspect of the feminine and not of the masculine, it does not have a need to move outwards, and when forced to do so it will exhaust both the one expressing it and the people around.

I have only emphasized on these differences between people, not in order to categorize them as good or bad, but because I find it useful to help identify these behaviors so that we can be more empathetic towards others and ourselves, and also choose the connections that are healthy and nurturing to us.

So, in conclusion to this short essay on joy, I would like to summarize the most important ideas:

- Joy is an inborn feminine attribute of humans, and it is

necessary to be aware of the tendency of our masculine aspect to overlook it.

- Laughter and celebration are natural manifestations of joy, and practicing them in a conscious and moderate way supports feminine energy.
- Being joyful has a strong impact on our interpersonal relationships and can have both a positive and a negative aspect that one should be aware of.
- Authentic joy is a vibration rather than an attitude; outer displays of false positivity are not a substitute for it and can represent a sign of unhealed trauma.

Chapter 7

Spirit

The realm of God, Love, and Intuition

I have titled this chapter *Spirit* to signify the totality of all that there is from the energetic perspective, both the Creator and creation itself in its nonphysical form. Many of you might believe in the concept of God, but there is a certain tendency to look at God as an individual being, a separate entity that is above all others. This is not in line with what is being described in this book, since everything in the Universe is connected, and the Creator is woven together with its creation.

Spirit is everything which is generated by God (or the source if you prefer this term), in its subtle form and not in physical form, and also includes the source itself. It is what the Christians refer to as the Holy Spirit, and the Hindus and Taoists as the Akashic dimension, or simply the Akasha. So what exactly is this *everything* in subtle form and what does it include, if not the physical aspect? Although a very simplified definition, it is the energetic and most divine component of all beings (which are all part of a single unit and not individualized as we might perceive it), and it is also information in its purest form. Many sources also refer to the Akashic records as a compendium of knowledge and information stored in the consciousness of all beings, but this term only describes the informational aspect of the dimension and disregards its living and being aspect. It is said that it comprises information on all that has happened and will happen in the future, however, this is an inaccurate description because linear time as we know it does not exist in the energetic dimension. Everything is actually happening in the present moment and although it is a difficult concept to grasp initially, I am only mentioning it for further reference.

But it is essentially information, which means that whatever you have felt and thought of, your experiences and memories, exist in that dimension permanently because they are all just information at their core. In other words, they can never be erased or undone. Intuition, wisdom, psychic events, telepathy, and other phenomena labelled as paranormal are all happening in the Akashic dimension. This is where we connect with the actual reality, which is the invisible and not the visible as we might imagine, since it is pure energy that gives birth to matter and not the other way around. When someone passes away, there is a tendency to refer to it as them going to *the other side*, but actually the other side is here, in the physical world which is just a projection of the energy. This is also why our existence in physical form is limited, as opposed to our existence as formless, energetic beings, which is permanent and endless. So we are just energetic beings having a limited human experience, and I always find it very comforting to remember because it helps put things into perspective.

I can imagine that by now some of you might wonder what God or this obscure dimension has to do with feminine energy. Because we all have the Akasha as an element or a part of us (which we sometimes identify as our soul or higher self), we are always connected to this field although we are mostly unaware of it. Out of our two polar aspects, it is the feminine which connects directly with it, and it does so firstly by intuition.

Intuition is the intelligence of the soul, just like the intellect is the intelligence of the physical brain. The first is feminine, the second is masculine. We are all accustomed and educated on using our physical brain, but how about intuition? Since the feminine is severely overlooked and suppressed in modern times, not surprisingly intuition suffers the same fate. It is generally accepted that women have intuition, but at the same time its use is often ridiculed or labelled as fantasy because it cannot be scientifically proven. For a very long time, we could not prove that the Earth spins around the Sun and not the other way around either, but nevertheless it is true; so there might come a time when intuition will also find its way in science books. But for that to happen, someone should first be opened to invest in the idea, and reconnecting with our feminine might be a good start.

It is safe to state that there are few people who have never had any instances in their lives when they just knew without being told, or they felt, that something has or will happen, that something is true or false, or that it is better to choose a certain option over another. This is how intuition works, or better said it should work, because most are tempted to ignore it or silence it altogether because it is not logical. Being in love or infatuated with someone is also not logical, but for some reason this does not prevent us from acting unreasonably on occasions. So why this need to explain intuition in order to follow it? Yes, perhaps it is unexplainable, but it is not absolutely necessary to explain everything at once. If it were, we would not be able to live with ourselves since we are barely able to understand a fraction of this Universe. I also do not understand completely how exactly a car works, but this does not prevent me from using it. Intuition is there to serve us when logic fails, not to replace it completely, as I also mentioned when discussing the reconciliation of the mental and the emotional bodies.

I believe that the most obvious obstacle preventing us from using intuition is the difficulty to distinguish it from imagination, which also makes us think they are one and the same, because it is just something happening inside our heads. This is true, but I would also point out the fact that if something goes on inside of us, that does not mean it is not real. Information coming from intuition can be distinguished from imagination by the fact that it does not follow any preexistent beliefs, habits and experiences, and is often completely unrelated to what we are doing and thinking in the moment we are receiving it. In other words, the more unexpected, the more likely it is intuition and not imagination. When we are imagining something, our line of thoughts follows established patterns: we imagine things that we are familiar with, that we like, or on the contrary, that usually give us anxiety, we make logical connections with previous experiences, and we are very much in our own persona. Intuitive insights, on the other hand, are not related to our personality and our memories at all, and tend to have no apparent explanation or logic. If you are deliberately thinking of a friend, you can imagine what they are doing at a certain time because you may know their habits and you can make assumptions based on previous experiences; if on the other hand, you are cooking dinner and suddenly get an image of them doing something seemingly unexpected, then that is most likely intuition. I encourage you to verify these insights when possible. In time, you will be able to tell the difference between your imagination and intuition. The feminine is a natural when it comes to telling one from another, which is why in ancient times, oracles (persons acting as a bridge between the seen and unseen world and having the gift of precognition) were more often than not female priestesses. The art of divination is also the realm of the feminine and is nothing more than connecting to the Akashic field (it is not foretelling the future, because the future simply does not exist, but it is picking up on an infinity of pieces of information and possibilities) by different means. Rarely do you see men involved in these practices; few are, but they are the ones who have developed their feminine side.

So in order to connect more to your intuition, try practices that silence your logical thinking, if only just for a few moments in the beginning, such as meditation. If you are not accustomed or do not resonate with it, grab a pen and a piece of paper and do some automatic writing (just right down the first thing that comes to mind, without filtering), or get a coloring book for adults, or draw your own mandalas. You will notice that with a bit of practice you will be able to empty your mind, so that information from Spirit can come in unhindered. It does not mean that you have to act on whatever information you receive; just be open and allow it in without judgement. It is certainly a skill that takes time to master, but we all have it in us and it is a great tool in discovering our own authenticity and truth, because the Akashic dimension is not subject to ego and to personal interpretations.

I was mentioning before that everything we have ever experienced and sensed, on every level, is recorded into this subtle field. From the energetic point of view, feeling or sensing is basically being into a certain vibration. We may perceive states of being as emotions, but essentially, they are also just energy, and the highest vibration of this energy is that of Love. This is the primordial vibration that gives birth to all others, the good and the bad. I have written it with a capital letter because I am not referring to human attachments or infatuations, but to divine Love. When we say that *God is Love,* a phrase you have certainly heard if you were ever in contact with religion, this is what we mean. Experiencing divine Love as humans in physical form is considerably difficult or impossible unless you are able to connect to Spirit, nevertheless you might experience earthly manifestations of it, which are inferior vibrations of Love. Caring for someone, being attached to them, feeling romantically connected to them, are all forms of Love. Having said that, once you have experienced love in any form, you have forever recorded it into the Akashic field, and since you are connected to it permanently, this means that love is always there for you. This is the real meaning of *Love never dies;* the energy itself is permanent, it is just us who disconnect from it and perceive it as having ended.

Since we live in a temporal dimension, where we perceive time as linear, it is somewhat normal to look at love in the same way. When that moment in time when we experienced love is gone, we also perceive it to be gone as well. It is always a cause of grief when we lose someone dear, whether to death or to other life circumstances, but this loss is not real. I am not inferring that grief is invalid or that it is wrong to feel this way, but it is also a consequence of us being disconnected from the higher dimension. By suppressing the real feminine in us, we have lost contact with our higher self that lives permanently in the vibration of Love. Therefore, women and people expressing a lot of feminine energy are more interested in all aspects of love, since they unconsciously seek to connect to the source of Love and of all that is. But not all hope is lost, and we can all remember how to connect to it again.

Firstly, you can try to go beyond the belief that emotions of any kind are just temporary chemical reactions in your brain and nothing more. This is a valid scientific fact, but only a part of the truth. Having at the back of your head the idea that when you feel something you actually generate energy that persists forever, is very useful when trying to reconnect to the higher realms. When a loving relationship of any kind ends, love does not end with it, and neither do negative emotions for that matter. Because as stated before, the past, present and future only exist in the physical world. I cannot imagine anybody consciously wanting to hold on to the negative emotions, but of course holding on to love is a different matter, because it is where we come from and wanting to go back to it is perfectly natural. So if you break up with someone or cease contact with a good friend, don't discard all the nice memories of them, neither symbolically nor physically. Keep objects that remind you of the good times, photographs and other tokens, and keep in mind that the good is still there, even if your physical experience might have turned sour at a certain point; this does not simply erase love. And when you finally become able to connect energetically to Spirit and to other people, you are able to experience that love again and any time you wish to, despite the passing of time or any physical obstacles.

Secondly, you can choose to be open to receiving new love, of whatever kind it may be: a friend reaching out to spend time together, receiving a gift from someone, or a compliment. I find that oftentimes we are reluctant to do so because we feel uncomfortable or find it unnecessary. The act of receiving is also a feminine attribute itself, and it is not for you to decide whether it is necessary or not. The person on the giving side obviously deemed it necessary, so appreciate it and give thanks. Feeling unworthy is the main obstacle in receiving, and being very well hidden deep within, this limiting belief is not easily identified. It also takes many different forms, so defining a certain behavior that would help identify this lack of self-worth in yourself and others is difficult, but one sign that you might be suffering from it is feeling bad and not knowing how to react when receiving something, or having a need to immediately compensate for the gesture (in other words feeling indebted). It is a limiting belief stemming from the fact that at a certain point in your life, most likely in childhood, you perceived love and often also abundance to be limited, or that love is only given on certain conditions (like being *good*, whatever the definition of it may have been). This belief runs in the family most of the time and it is not surprising, since we tend to replicate the relationship we had with our parents into our relationships with our children.

Every transaction in the physical world of objects, gestures and emotions has an energetic component to it and can ultimately be reduced down to Love. I am not referring to business transactions (although they also have an energetic dynamic), but to personal ones where we are emotionally invested in some way. So, in order to connect to Love as a vibration and keep it flowing, it is necessary to also express it in the physical by allowing the giving and the receiving (the masculine and the feminine) and when you are accustomed to receiving easily, you are also willing to give unrestricted. This can be sometimes hard when there is no trust between people, and while it is true that there might be a hidden agenda behind a certain gesture from someone, there is no need to focus on this matter when receiving. You can still be open to receive simply as an act of love for yourself, regardless of the giver's intent, as long as you are aware that receiving Love is unconditional on the energetic plane but can be considered conditional in the 3D world, if not by you then perhaps by the other. To put it in different words, treat all your transactions as being energetic rather than physical and let the other person make whatever they like out of them. If they are disconnected from their higher self and secretly expect to receive back, then the relationship is energetically misbalanced and will eventually end, whether you want it to or not. And if it does, perhaps it is for the better. Naturally, the above discussion does not apply to giving or receiving extreme gestures, or to immoral and illegal activities, so use your good judgement in addition to your intuition. If there are signs of a transaction being fundamentally wrong or toxic, do not engage in it.

So Spirit is where all good and real things happen and also where our true legacy as human beings is stored. While we might accomplish things on Earth (and it is natural to do so), it is useful to keep in mind that they are all just temporary, including giving birth to a child, which some might consider as the utmost accomplishment. It is not my intention to minimize the importance of any earthly goals, but only point out that they are merely a small part of what we generate in a lifetime, and certainly not the part that will persist eventually. Only when we connect to Spirit can we live in the vibration of love and truth and we can be fulfilled just by existing, without chasing for ephemeral incentives in the physical world.

As usual, I will summarize the main message of this section:

- Spirit, or the Akasha, is the nonphysical aspect of all that exists in the Universe and includes the higher self of all beings and all information in its purest form.

- The Akashic field is a realm of timeless and endless energy, and is the source of what happens in the physical Universe.
- The feminine is connected to Spirit by intuition, an essential attribute that allows us to pull information from higher realms and that can be developed with practice.
- The primordial vibration of Spirit is Love.
- We have the possibility to permanently connect to Love through our feminine aspect.

Chapter 8

Nurturing

Making small things big

The act of nurturing, or the attribute of being a nurturer, has always been associated with the feminine. Ever since humans started living together in families and social groups, it was the women that were looking after the children and the sick and attending to their immediate needs, such as giving food and medicine, warmth and anything else they could not get on their own. The standard definition of the verb *to nurture* is mainly to encourage the development of something or someone, and especially of children. However, there are also other aspects to this term which are not immediately made obvious by this definition and which I think are worth mentioning.

The first thing that should be pointed out is that the act of nurturing can take two forms: one is nurturing the self and the other is nurturing someone else, and I find that oftentimes the first form is completely ignored, which is why it is also not apparent in the dictionaries either. We are tempted to only direct it externally because this is what the definition suggests, so I prefer defining it as *making small things big*, as mentioned in the title, because it is not pointed towards anyone or anything in particular. At a closer look, I think this description really does summarize the concept, regardless of what it is applied to: a human being, a plant, a business, a skill etc. Everyone has things which they might want to grow, both in themselves and in others; if you have a small amount of money, you want to make it higher, and if your child has a certain talent, you might want to help them develop it. So there is no difference between looking after ourselves and attending to other people's needs when it comes to this act of nurturing. Both sides reside in the feminine spectrum of energy, so if we want to have a healthy and balanced feminine, we should strive to address both.

So what exactly is there to nurture in yourself and how to do it? First, identify what it is in you or in your life that feels too small. When I say that something is too small, I mean that there is an imbalance, and one should always stay aware of their imbalances. If you perceive your work-life balance as unsuitable at any time point, for instance if you feel that you do not get enough downtime, the obvious next step would be to *attend* to your time. If you have too little energy, make the effort to nourish your energy levels by doing something that relaxes and replenishes you; this might mean taking time from other activities. We always instinctively know what exactly is missing, but we are either unconscious of it because we are too busy to pay attention to ourselves, or we are simply not accustomed to doing so. Many perceive it as being selfish, but I personally do not see how an exhausted person can look properly after someone in need. Or better said, I have seen it and I can honestly say that most of the time it does not end up well for either of the parties. As mentioned before in this book, only someone whose cup is filled has enough to give out of. So sit with yourself at least from time to time, if not on a regular basis, and think whether there is something beneficial to you which you would like to make or have more of, and before thinking of exchanging your small boat with a yacht, start with the basic needs. Basic needs may vary from person to person, but they are generally proper diet, rest, safety, health, connecting to others, expressing oneself, being joyful etc. You can put anything on the list that you consider essential for your well-being and happiness. And if you are to be completely honest with yourself, you will also come to the conclusion that you have quite a few basic needs which you are not attending to properly. Of course, some of those things may not be exclusively dependent on you, but they still are to a certain extent. If you spend too much time working and do not have time to rest, you might not be able to fix it right away by finding another job, but when you do have some time, do you actually rest, or are you involved in other activities? Are those activities really that important and cannot be missed (e.g., do you really need to socialize when you would rather sleep, or do you need to do the cleaning right away)? Can they not wait? I kept using the word *need*, to emphasize that very often we just want things but do not need them.

Once you've identified the imbalance that you want fixed, a helpful next step would be to stop feeling guilty or ashamed for nurturing yourself. As a note, when we perceive that we have betrayed our own standards, we feel guilt, and when we have betrayed other people's standards, we feel shame. And I feel guided to mention it because I found that it is an extremely common tendency, caused partly by a misunderstanding of the concept of selflessness, and partly by the excessive expression of masculine energy.

Being selfless means being more concerned with the needs of others than one's own, and it is a virtue, but it does not mean that living in a permanent state of it is healthy or normal. Sometimes, doing too much is just as damaging as not doing enough, not to mention that for some nothing is ever good enough, no matter how much of ourselves we are willing to give. So, establishing healthy boundaries is necessary so that we do not end up depleting ourselves energetically or emotionally. Mothers, and especially of newborns and toddlers, often fall into the habit of feeling guilty for just about anything they do for themselves that doesn't include the child. Taking 30 minutes for a bath after a long day is unthinkable when you can take a three-minute shower. Even though young children might need supervision 24/7, they don't necessarily need their mother 24/7 (I am not suggesting leaving them unattended, but rather ask and accept help from others around, if and whenever possible).

As to the other source of shame and guilt, which is relying

excessively on masculine energy, this issue is a little more complex. The masculine craves appreciation for doing things, above anything else; when this energy is unbalanced and there is no self-appreciation coming from within as well, this goal is never achieved. You will always be concerned with what others think of you, always compare yourself to someone that has more or is more, so there is never any time and energy left to nurture yourself. Validation becomes more important than any of your basic needs. The feminine, on the other side, does not need to prove anything (and in its most exalted state, not even to the self), which is why maintaining a good balance between the two is so essential. If you find that you have the tendency to be concerned by what others think of you, then you are not honoring your feminine. This does not mean that being in your feminine energy is disregarding common sense and manners or crossing other people's boundaries; it just means that justifying things that you do, like nurturing yourself, is not necessary. Attending to your basic needs is not something you have to earn or explain yourself for, and if the environment you are in is not accepting of these needs, then it is advisable to change it. It is more difficult when the lack of acceptance comes from family members, but most of the time, we can make certain choices of environment, for instance of the social or professional one.

Another thing I would like to discuss with respect to nurturing is the necessity to prioritize needs over wants. In other words, what exactly do we nurture first? A good rule of thumb for distinguishing needs from wants is that a need is very personal and does not refer to specific people or objects in the external environment. When there is a need to feel safe for instance, it can be fulfilled by a number of different things, such as living in any house that offers the feeling of protection from the outside world or being around caring people who you can rely on. It is not only *that* house, or *that* person who can make you feel safe. When there is a need for financial stability, it could be fulfilled by a number of jobs, not just one. So if you notice that this sense of lack is only connected to a very specific thing or person, then that is a want and therefore always comes second. This discrimination is especially useful when we nurture children since they cannot make this distinction for themselves. Also, as opposed to a need, which cannot be substituted with anything, wanting something means having a preference for it, therefore a want can be substituted. If you have a need to spend time in nature in order to relax, then you will never be fully relaxed until you do so. You can choose to do it by renting out a bigger or a smaller cabin in the woods, and although you might want (have a preference for) the bigger one, you cannot say that choosing the smaller will prevent you from relaxing. So in order to be able to nurture yourself properly, it is also helpful to identify more than one way to satisfy a need and choose or prioritize whatever is possible or easier at the time.

Having discussed how to address personal needs, I am now moving on to the topic of interpersonal relationships and nurturing other people. As mentioned before, nurturing is making small things big; having said that, adults are already *big* as a manner of speech, so humans, and especially women, are not here to nurture adults which are fully able to fend for themselves. And here I would like to emphasize on how not filling our cups and not nurturing ourselves leads to us exhausting others with no regard for their own well-being. This is applicable for both genders and is especially the case for people who are disconnected from their feminine energy, who look to compensate for it externally and end up having codependent relationships with people who express enough of it, such as their mothers, or wives (or better yet, both). I once had a colleague who turned up late at work on a Monday and explained that although she had ironed ten shirts for her husband during the weekend, he did not want to wear any of them, so she decided to iron the eleventh one for him although she was already running late. This is an example of how not being willing to look after ourselves puts an unnecessary burden on other people, and especially on those who feel a sense of obligation to nurture others while disregarding themselves, and oftentimes are also educated as such. Not liking to cook or prepare meals is perfectly acceptable, but as an adult, not being willing to even try to fulfill such a basic need for oneself and always expecting others do it, is being completely disconnected from the feminine aspect. Also, being open to do acts of service for someone is an expression of love and appreciation, but being forced into doing so by more or less insidious means, no longer counts as nurturing. Nurturing is something that we do willingly and is not a profession or an obligation. Moreover, when we are providing all of the feminine energy in a relationship because the other party has none, this relationship becomes codependent.

At the other end of the spectrum, we may have an inability to nurture people around us, often defined as being selfish, which also comes from not owning or not expressing enough healthy feminine energy. Helping something or someone to grow in a certain respect might require a number of resources, but most of the time it is more about investing time and energy rather than material resources, although both categories are important. When we are reluctant to invest, it is generally because we perceive the investment to lead to a lack for ourselves, because we might end up having less of whatever the resource is. While this can be true in some cases, oftentimes it only reflects an imbalance that we have not yet fixed. If we are reluctant to give our time for example, it is because we perceive that we do not have enough for ourselves and this in itself should be a warning sign that we have an unmet need. Again, it circles back to self-nourishing, so attending to our own needs should come first if we want to have something to share in the first place.

From the practical perspective, there are a few methods which I find useful in keeping a good balance between nourishing the self and others. One of them, mentioned briefly before, is identifying your needs. Start by making a list of your basic and immediate needs, without being judgmental towards them (just because something is considered unnecessary or shameful by your family or social circle, it does not mean it is not right for you to need it). Inhibiting or ignoring a need will not make it disappear; on the contrary it will feed it and especially its darker side, so be honest and accept yourself as you are. As I mentioned before, you do not have to justify yourself for everything either. Then write next to each of them, whether it is met fully, only partially or completely unmet. Obviously, the ones which are completely unmet should be addressed first, followed by the second category. For each one of these, identify at least two ways of nurturing it (remember there is always more than one way to fulfill a need, otherwise it is classified as a want). For instance, if you realized that you need to socialize more, you could do that by initiating contact with your friends more, meeting new people by attending events, workshops or picking up a new hobby, or coming up with ideas of new social activities to propose to friends and family. Needs and wants can change over time, so this is an exercise that can be repeated regularly. It is not necessary to write down every time, once you get in the habit of knowing yourself better, it will come naturally; and once you gain confidence that you are able to fulfill your own needs, you will also be more open to nurturing others.

Another exercise is analyzing whether you are critical towards others nurturing themselves in any way. While you might not share the same perspective on life and well-being, resistance to witnessing other people attending to their needs is a sign that you are not comfortable with your feminine energy. If a friend cancels a lunch appointment with you simply because they are too tired (so they are just looking after their immediate needs) and you feel resentment towards it, it is very likely because you do not nurture yourself enough either. Not allowing yourself to put your basic needs before social or professional commitments out of a sense of obligation, makes you become judgmental towards others doing so. Otherwise, you would have been understanding towards them, even though the event might be inconvenient for you. So being kind to ourselves is essential and helps to be more accepting of others as well.

In conclusion, I am summarizing below the most important aspects of this basic feminine quality of being nurturing:

- Nurturing involves attending to both ourselves and to others, in equal proportions.
- Nurturing oneself is identifying an unmet need and restoring the inner balance by attending to it.
- Feelings of shame and guilt are a major obstacle in expressing the feminine and therefore in fulfilling our own personal needs.
- Self-nurturing is essential for maintaining well-balanced relationships and for being able to look after others as well.

Chapter 9

Compassion

Seeing Oneself in Another

I have spoken about how we are all connected on the energetic level and about the oneness we share in Spirit, and also mentioned that it takes a certain amount of awareness to experience it consciously. Even though we may not be in the optimal state to perceive this connection, or not always, compassion is given to us to experience it on a basic and earthly level. Compassion is generally understood as feeling concern for someone going through a difficult time or wanting to help them, and it is nothing but a result of this spiritual oneness expressing itself in the physical reality. Naturally, the more compassion we are able to experience, the closer we are to becoming aware of our link to Spirit.

Compassion is often confused with expressing emotion when confronted with others' misfortunes, so it is easy to label expressive people as being compassionate and kind, and more introverted ones with being the opposite, and I would like to clarify this confusion first. The level of someone's expressiveness is just a measure of how extroverted they are, and not of how compassionate they can be. In fact, it is the introverts that experience a closer connection to Spirit, so it is likely that they are more affected by people's suffering than the extroverts but are less comfortable with showing it. I agree that a kind word is very helpful to someone in need, but this tendency to value the wrapping over the content leads to a world where everyone sheds tears for the suffering, but nobody does anything. So, it is not that much about our ability to express, but about our willingness to act on it.

The connection to the spiritual realm is, as previously

mentioned, the domain of the feminine. When we are aware that who we are at our core is our soul and not the ego (the persona we have built for ourselves with the help of education and social conventions), and that we are not separated from other beings just because we have separate physical bodies, we are in our feminine energy. The feminine sees beyond appearance and realizes that all beings are different expressions of the Divine, regardless of how they choose or are conditioned to present themselves. So when somebody else is in any kind of pain, we are as well, and not giving them a helping hand would essentially equal not doing anything for ourselves, since we are all one. The extent to which the feminine has been suppressed becomes therefore obvious in the lack of compassion the modern world suffers from, despite the political correctness at surface level, and causes armed conflicts, massive segregation between the rich and the poor, destructive acts against the planet, class and racial favoritism etc. This is not a choice of mine to be negative by focusing on these aspects instead of the good, it is a quantifiable fact. Our society being predominantly patriarchal, men occupy most positions of authority and power, and this in itself is not a problem; the issue is that a lot of them are out of tune with their feminine aspect, so compassion is usually not on their list of priorities, and oftentimes on any list at all.

So let's discuss what lack of compassion is; according to the definition mentioned above, the opposite would be either not feeling concern or sadness with regard to others, or not wishing to do anything about it, and both of them are equally impactful. Not feeling is a natural state of being for those cut off from their feminine energy, and it is not necessarily the inability to feel but the tendency to inhibit it. All beings have emotional bodies, so it cannot be that one was born with the inability to feel (pathological cases are a result of malfunctions of the mind and physical bodies, not of the emotional one). This behavior is acquired through education and sometimes it is a method of protection from life experiences perceived as negative, so it is the realm of the ego and not of the soul. In other words, it is a mask one puts on in order to be able to cope, and it is understandable to a certain extent. Considering the dysfunctional model of masculinity that most men nowadays have been raised with, and the amount of pressure that comes with positions of power, it is not surprising that they tend to inhibit emotions. This, however, is an explanation and not an excuse, since acquired beliefs can be changed if there is a willing for it. Of course, the above is applicable to both genders equally, but I have chosen men as an example because the adversity to feeling is more common and obvious with them, and so are its effects on society.

The ego is mostly constructed as a protective mechanism already very early in life, and the lack of compassion is one facet of this ego. During the first years of life, we first become aware of ourselves (of our needs, experiences and feelings), before becoming aware of the outside world. Since the first pain we feel as youngsters is our own pain, whether that is physical or caused by a perceived lack of attention or affection, the resistance to feeling and to emotion is all about us and our inner universe. It might be triggered by outside events, but it is pointed inwards. Therefore, before discussing compassion towards others, we should discuss self-compassion (we must be able to see ourselves first before identifying the same in another). If we have initially turned the compassion switch off because of our own resistance to suffering, then we can also turn it on by resolving this resistance.

Blocking out emotions can be very convenient for a while, but from the energetic perspective it represents the inhibition of feminine energy, and as mentioned when discussing the topic of flow, the feminine does not react well when restrained. Everyone intuitively knows this, which is why we are afraid that once letting go, we will not be able to stop the flow of emotions or control it, and that we will ultimately not be able to cope. The more we try to keep it under control, the more violent it will be when it is finally released, but keeping it inside is not an option; like a moving body of water, in time it erodes every shore and rock it encounters. Physically, this means illness, if not a serious one than at least a long array of uncomfortable symptoms that reduce life standards and are difficult to manage. The organs which are most affected by the inhibition of emotions and feelings are the liver, the stomach, and the gut. Not surprisingly, people who suffer from irritable bowel syndrome and some liver disorders are more affected by their symptoms before or during stressful events which trigger some amount of emotion. So, let your emotions come out, and especially the negative ones (this does not mean taking it out on others, but expressing them). You cannot be compassionate towards something you have not witnessed, so you must first feel yourself whatever there is to be compassionate about: grief, frustration, anger, sadness, indignation, and any other perfectly normal human expressions. Taking it out on other people only happens because you are suppressing emotions instead of expressing them, and these two activities are not equivalent; you can be expressive without being damaging to other people. Talk about things with a friend or a professional, keep a journal or simply admit to yourself that you are experiencing unpleasant feelings and write them down on a piece of paper. You can even burn the paper afterwards, as a symbolic gesture of release, but also for privacy reasons if you are uncomfortable with others knowing of it. If you have got to a stage where these emotions have become extreme, for instance after a very traumatic event or after keeping them inside for a long time, then these methods might not be sufficient. You might also need to express them in a more extreme way, such as crying, shouting, or just taking it out on a pillow (you can do it when you are alone and in a safe environment, since sharing it with others might be a source of additional inhibition). Needless to say, if you have been through very distressful and traumatic events, then it is advisable to ask for professional help. But in fairly normal life circumstances, it is safe to choose one of the above methods and not leave your pain unattended until it reaches apocalyptic dimensions. And I think everyone can vouch from their own experience how cathartic a good cry can be at times.

When we allow ourselves to feel and express negative emotions as we experience them, we also have less of a tendency to identify ourselves with them, in other words we become more comfortable with them coming and going. There will be no need to judge and to hold on to feelings, so our perception of the misfortune of others also changes for the better. It is easier to understand something we have also been through, which is also a reason why most people become more empathetic with age. So this is why I say that the journey to being kind or compassionate to others starts with acting the same towards ourselves. That is not to say that adopting self-pity as a lifestyle is constructive and I am certainly not endorsing the victim status, but we can be more allowing of ourselves to feel both the good and the bad as part of life.

As I stated before, seeing and accepting who we are without judgement helps see the same in others and helps develop the sense of oneness which I was discussing at the beginning of this chapter. Even though people might have essentially different life experiences, ultimately it all comes down to a few very basic human emotions or states of being, which we all go through, consciously or not. Two experiences might be apparently different, but they might elicit the same type of response after all (someone who grew up without their parents may experience a sense of abandonment and so will someone who lost a loved one or has gone through a divorce later in life). It is not necessary to be terribly similar to someone in order to be compassionate towards them. Validating and being respectful of these basic states of being in us and others is what compassion is actually about. It is not being vocal about it, so if you tell a friend about your difficult day and they don't talk much back, don't assume they are uncaring or insensitive; holding space for someone and just listening is also a show of respect towards their feelings. Women are more comfortable with sharing experiences and communicating, which is not necessarily the case in men and generally people with a lot of masculine energy. This is also why men are not inclined to speak to each other about negative experiences; firstly, they judge themselves for having emotions (since this is perceived as a sign of weakness), and secondly, they do not really know what to say. But as I mentioned above, feedback is not always required when being compassionate, so men can also learn how to hold space for each other and they should, if they strive for inner balance.

Moving on from the feeling part, the willingness part of compassion is also important. So when you feel sympathy for yourself or another, are you actually doing something about it? Doing does not necessary refer to grand gestures or donating money, but also to trivial things, such as stop blaming others (and yourself) for having reached this state, enquiring after them or offering to do a small act of service of any kind, such as buying or bringing them something. If neither is possible, then sending them good thoughts is also an option, since thoughts are forms of energy (this does not mean that you will magically make things better for them, but it does have a positive impact on them on an energetic level, if they are open to receive). If you do not feel compelled to do anything, then you might just be emotional about the situation and not compassionate, and if this is the case, there is also no need to feel guilty about it. Being aware of it and accepting it in the first place is a good place to start, and oftentimes this in itself is so healing that you will notice your compassion gradually and naturally growing in time. When I was very young, I used to hold myself to a certain standard of compassion and kindness due to the religious environment I was brought up in, but somehow it never worked for me. I always felt it was an imposed and artificial kindness, and when I decided to do things on my own terms and in my own time, it helped me be much more compassionate in an authentic way. So if others are more sympathetic or empathetic than you, and they do more for others, it's all right, it doesn't make you less valuable as a person; it just means that you can find your own way of making a difference.

One other aspect to beware of is the tendency to victimize oneself or others, and this is a highly sensitive topic. How do we know if someone is dealing with an inconvenient situation that takes time to resolve, or they are just experiencing the victim status? Usually, the more defensive people are about their situation, the more of a victim status they are trying to acquire. If someone is in the habit of becoming resentful or aggressive when you try to make them see the glass as being half full instead of half empty, or when you enquire about what has been done to overcome the tricky situation or offer some advice, then they are in the victim mentality. In this case, trying to do something for them is pointless, since they will not be ready to leave the victim seat no matter how hard you try. Being a victim can be extremely validating for some and in time it becomes an addictive way of living, in which case it is safe to stop doing anything and even stop feeling compassionate about them altogether. This does not mean you are being insensitive or cruel; victimization feeds on the energy of compassion like nothing else and fuelling this black hole will not serve anyone, on the contrary. You would be better off, in this case, redirecting your energy towards someone who is truly in need, while still respecting or loving the one who chooses the victim status since their choice does not make them less deserving.

Having said that, anyone can have a tendency to be a victim at times, including yourself. This is in fact one of the shadow sides (also called shadow archetype) of the feminine and I often assimilate it to the story of Rapunzel, although there are many other myths and folk stories based on a main female character (the princess) who is a victim of the villain, and a male character (the prince) who is trying to save her. Of course, having to face difficult and uncomfortable situations in life is a fact and I am not trying to minimize or ridicule this, but you might be tempted to place power outside of you instead of taking action to make things better for yourself. In the above example, the shadow archetype would be the one of the damsel in distress who doesn't actually take any action but enjoys being passive and receiving the help and sympathy of others. So, next time you encounter an obstacle, or you are faced with a distressful situation, first ask yourself if there is anything you can do to make it better, even though this might not constitute an immediate solution per se. If not, asking for advice or help is also healthy; however, just talking about it and being passive is not, at least not in the long term.

To summarize, I am outlining what I find to be the most important aspects related to compassion:

- Compassion is the earthly reflection of the oneness we all share in Spirit, and it is our feminine side which helps us connect and see ourselves in others.
- Resistance to feeling our own emotions leads to difficulty in being compassionate towards others and it can be overcome by accepting and expressing any negative feelings we might be experiencing.
- Compassion is seeing and respecting in others a fundamental state of being which we might have experienced in different circumstances.
- Compassion is not only witnessing and feeling, but also being willing to do something about it.
- Victimization is fuelled by compassion but is not resolved by it, therefore being aware of this behavior in us and

others is useful in maintaining healthy relationships, including with ourselves.

Chapter 10

Lightness of Heart

The ability to put things into perspective

I have purposefully saved this topic for last, after talking about things which might be considered more serious or of more consequence, such as love, health, manifestation, or God. However, it is not less important; on the contrary, it is an essential theme to have in mind and which can help us go through everyday life if not in a more joyful way, at least with a bit more peace of mind. Lightness of heart can mean many things, but ultimately, it means not taking yourself or life too seriously. Perhaps not the easiest thing to do when going through turmoil, but I find that even in less stressful and routine situations, it is the first on the list to be forgotten.

I remember when growing up, especially while going through schooling, that we would often become agitated about things like assignments or exams, and from time to time an adult would point out how these are not actual reasons to be stressed about and that there are more important things in life. Needless to say, it took a few years of growing up until I fully understood and got to share their point of view. But funnily enough, I realized that one never actually finalizes this process of learning what exactly is important, or as I wrote in the title, of learning how to put things into perspective. Not taking yourself too seriously does not mean disregarding what you are experiencing, but rather getting into the habit of looking at it as something you just go through, without the temptation of setting a big goal behind it or putting an impressive label on it. Not everything that happens has a dramatic impact on you as a timeless and formless expression of the Divine, and I dare say that very few things do. It is just the ego that becomes excessively attached to goals or to certain fabricated perceptions of what life is or should be, which inadvertently leads to heartache or even despair, and one should remember that, after all, everything is just temporary.

Since I already mentioned goals, let us talk about why we need to set them, and ultimately, if we need them at all. The mere status of being, of existing, implies that there must be a purpose to it, or at least prompts to the question of why we exist in the first place. Since the topic of this chapter is lightness of heart, I will not go into philosophy and I will also admit that I do not have a definite answer to the question, nor do I believe that anyone else does. But what if there is no other purpose to life than just living and enjoying it? Just like we cannot prove that there is a goal, we cannot disprove this hypothesis either, so it is worth taking it into consideration. Because we perceive time as linear, we also see the idea of living as heading into a specific direction without being able to hold still or go back; it must be that it is going somewhere so better define what that *somewhere* is, before it is too late. This is the basic reason we set goals: to give significance and a destination to our journey. But as I mentioned earlier, in the realm of energy, time is actually not linear and there is nothing else except the present moment; so if time isn't going anywhere, perhaps life isn't a one-way track either.

Having goals is useful and makes one feel of value; it is an expression of masculine energy that wants to do and accomplish, and it is advisable to let this energy express itself. Without it, there probably would not even be an organized Universe. But feminine energy is the one that remembers that beyond all this, it just *is* and will never cease to *be*, and that whatever goal is being set, whether it is reached or not, will never change this. So in the grand scheme of things, nothing is actually as essential as it appears to be. Considering how focused we are on our masculine aspect, it is not surprising that the thought of our goals not being that important, or of not having any, often gives rise to indignation or stagger; if you find that it is also the case for you, then you are not honoring your feminine enough. Achieving a balance between the masculine and the feminine means setting and following goals without becoming attached to them; better said, wanting things and striving to be someone is all very well as long as failure does not become distressful. Of course, one will not rejoice in not being able to achieve something, but it does not follow that this is a reason to feel less valuable or less happy. If you have set a target for yourself to be somewhere else in the near future in terms of skills, income or relationship status, which has not been reached, if you wanted a promotion but did not get it or wanted to achieve mastery in a certain domain and you feel that you have not, don't judge yourself for it. It is not always about the destination, sometimes it is just about the journey, and even though you have not got to where you think you should be, you have still grown in certain respects. You can still celebrate yourself for the effort put in and for the lessons learned, and you should. And perhaps life has other plans for you around the corner, that might prove to be just as good or better in the long run.

I cannot discuss goals without also approaching the concept of ambition, which means the will and determination to achieve something. Certainly, a useful trait to have but also dangerous because being overly focused on a target prevents us from seeing into perspective. That lightness of heart is completely obliterated on the way to achieve whatever it is that is deemed necessary. So where is this ambition coming from, or better said, who determines what it is appropriate to be ambitious about? One might naturally say that it is a personal choice, but is it really or is it just projected by society? Many of us are first raised in the belief that we should be ambitious about higher education, then no sooner have we graduated than it is expected from us to get a job and keep moving up the ladder. Then once we have attained a certain stability we are suggested that starting a family is the appropriate thing to do. That is not to say that there is anything wrong with any of these, but make sure you do things because you genuinely want them, not because you are measuring yourself against someone else's standards. So being ambitious about what makes you happy instead of what makes others happy is a good distinction to make in the first place. And I feel especially guided to emphasize this to men feeling pressured to perform or provide in order to prove their worth, and to women being pushed to marry and have children because what else is there to life for a woman. If you are unable to be light at heart despite your efforts, then perhaps you are following other people's goals or are letting them assess your value with their own currency.

Putting things into perspective is not only important when doing, but also when experiencing and feeling. And here we come to the topic of how to be lighthearted despite what we are going through, and especially the bad. As mentioned before, everything is just temporary and the waiting itself is also temporary, even if it seems to last for a very long time. If nothing lasts forever, it means that there will be a time when you will be free of this unpleasant experience (in one way or another), so how much is it then worth to dwell on? Of course, sometimes it is so bad that it is difficult to wait through it, but I find that these instances in life are not that common and certainly do not happen every day. Unless you are going through a terrible illness or hardship, I think it is safe to state that most days we should be able to be lighthearted. As a disclaimer, reaching this lightness of heart is a process and not a sudden realization, and once there, it is not necessarily a permanent state of being but it is rather a habit (much like being in the habit of having coffee at 10 o'clock in the morning, there might be days when there is no possibility for it), and one can always find a way to go back to it.

So how to know if you are lighthearted or not? As mentioned

previously, it is very difficult to be lighthearted permanently, but you can get accustomed to being aware of yourself when you are not in that state of mind so that you can try to shift your perspective. Generally, a sensible way of telling is by evaluating the amount of negative everyday emotions experienced, and also their intensity. For instance, having a small amount of stress at work is fairly normal most of the time, but if that stress spills into other sectors of your life or invades your weekends and holidays making you think of work, then you are not lighthearted. If you are worried about an important upcoming event or examination as opposed to just being focused, you are not being lighthearted. If you become irritated about occasionally doing things you don't like or being in places and with people you are not comfortable with, even though it is only for short periods of time, then you are again not lighthearted. Putting things into perspective is being able to accept and even appreciate small unpleasant moments for the sake of the bigger picture and oftentimes just because they are provisional, and also not giving things more importance than they deserve. Giving things too much importance leads to the fear of losing them, and fear in itself is the opposite of lightness. So we could also say that having lightness of heart is not being fearful of current or future events. We become overly worried, angry, frustrated, and sad for instance for fear of losing a job or a partnership of any kind, or one's reputation, as if there is no life beyond these. There is always someone or something beyond, provided we trust ourselves and are open to this possibility. If you are under the impression of knowing that the future can only bring something worse or less valuable, this is called negative thinking and it will not serve you well, even if you end up proving you were right in the first place.

The importance of this capacity to take things lightly only starts to become obvious towards the end of life here, when one starts wishing that they had been more appreciative and less bothered of what they were or had, since the clock of the earthly existence has started to tick. And this I have heard from too many elderlies to ignore, so let us learn from our forbearers and enjoy life now rather than later. For some reason, *later* never seems to rise to our expectations and it might not even be there, so postponing the lightness of heart until tomorrow does not make a lot of sense. If you have not made a conscious decision to be lighthearted so far, you can still do it; this choice only will already make a lot of difference.

Besides having wisdom (which we all have, although not to the same extent or it might sometimes come at a later stage in life), being playful also helps to not take things too seriously. Playfulness is something adults rarely keep in their closets, and it is a pity because their inner child is still there, waiting to be entertained. Some might seem to be more naturally inclined to express it, and although I agree that we are all different, we were all children at a certain point and some things never change (our inner child is always with us energetically because it never stops existing in the Akashic field, it is just another version of us that also wants to be acknowledged). So a good place to start is literally playing from time to time, whatever we enjoy and suits us: a sport, a board game, a playful outdoor activity, an escape room or a craft workshop, or simply drawing or dancing. We can always find something we like and that can also become a hobby, as long as we allow ourselves to indulge without feeling ashamed or labelling it in any way. I once heard a man saying that although he is very comfortable with his masculinity, he really enjoys sewing but feels embarrassed to admit it. Along the same line, I have to say that I enjoy occasionally playing hide and seek with my cat despite being well beyond the proper age for it, but I feel no shame in admitting it whatsoever.

I realize men might have more resistance in accepting such things because of the social prejudice, so they would rather stay on the safe side with football, fishing, or video games.

Unfortunately, even that is often labelled as childish and unnecessary, so I would like to emphasize on how harmful abstaining completely from such playful behavior is. By doing so, we are completely denying a side of ourselves and classifying it as improper, and in time this will inevitably grow into frustration and even extreme behavior. The so-called middle-aged crisis is also partially triggered by the total inhibition of the inner child, and while I do not endorse playing video games excessively or being irresponsible either, all adults need to occasionally take refuge from daily life and allow their inner child to vent. Women, on the other hand (and especially more feminine ones), are a little more playful generally and might express themselves more, even if just by not being too serious and getting together over a coffee and simply laughing about things. So, it is important that both genders make some room for this lightness of heart in their own way, and any healthy relationship must be able to accommodate it.

Lightness of heart is a feminine attribute because it allows us, among other things, to nurture and connect to our inner child (as stated in the previous chapter, the act of nurturing is feminine). Children are usually not taken very seriously, since it is the adults that know better, and perhaps they do most of the time, but not always. Adults often do not connect to children in the real sense, because connecting implies that the two halves of the picture are somewhat at the same level, and in real life they tend to position themselves as superior to their offspring, at least in terms of setting the priorities. Of course, it is the responsibility of the parent to guide and look after the well-being of the child since they cannot do it for themselves, but this might, at least on occasion, turn into disregard towards the child's authenticity. I am not stating that all parents do this, and certainly during the last decade or so there has been more awareness on the topic. What I would like to point out is that our relationship with our children is strictly dependent on that which we have with our own inner child. The inability to be lighthearted prevents us from acknowledging and nurturing the inner child properly, so it is unlikely that we will do so when it comes to our actual children (as within, so without). If we do manage to connect authentically to them with some psychological assistance, at the least we might not be able to enjoy parenthood enough. This is the reason why some parents are most of the time stressed and why some children are in the habit of throwing massive tantrums every other day, and not surprisingly since they don't really feel heard and seen. So, if you experience any of the above very often, or you are just contemplating the idea of becoming a parent, check on your relationship with your inner child first.

Having lightness of heart is, in a way, having the ability to see life through the eyes of a child, as well as of an adult, and as mentioned above, we are both at the same time. This is not possible unless we honor our inner child, and it means on one side acknowledging that they are still there, and on the other side, being compassionate towards them. If you have the tendency to be melancholic about your childhood, or on the contrary do not remember or don't want to remember it, then it could be that you are not honoring that past version of yourself, so it will be difficult to be lighthearted. So, a particularly useful exercise is to relax or lay down somewhere you will not be disturbed and go back in time by accessing memories from your childhood, good and bad. You will be surprised by what comes up, including things which you thought you had forgotten. Stay with your memories and emotions and allow them to fill you up, even if they might be incredibly sad (oftentimes people cry, which is a good thing because they are connecting with a side of themselves that needs compassion). There is no need to judge anyone or provide explanations to yourself in this process, because as already established in the previous chapter, compassion is just holding space for yourself and validating your experiences and feelings, and those of others as well. Whatever your reactions and feelings as a child, they were perfectly normal and there is no need to deny them or feel guilty. Spend as long as you need in this state and repeat, if necessary, until the memories stop triggering a strong emotional reaction. This exercise is not a substitute for therapy in cases of severe childhood trauma, but it does help to relieve a certain type of trauma, which is the denial of some aspects of the self; in other words, it helps us be more complete. It is also a good start for inner work and other types of therapy; your inner child will let you know if they need professional help.

From a practical perspective, I would like to summarize the essential ideas discussed in this chapter:

- Lightness of heart is the habit of not taking life too seriously and can be achieved by staying aware of the transience of all things and also by being playful.
- Setting goals and being ambitious, as expressions of the masculine, should be balanced with lightness of heart as an expression of the feminine.
- Our inner child is permanently a part of us, and is in need of acknowledgment and connection.
- Disregarding our inner child prevents us from embracing life lightheartedly.

Final Thoughts

The ten principles of the feminine described here can potentially be used as a manual on how to become more feminine, but not necessarily as per the socially accepted norm, since they are meant to offer a broader perspective on what being feminine means. As we have learned here, the feminine is not about what we wear or about choosing to display certain feminine behaviors, these being just a small sector of life where feminine energy might express itself, and then again it might not. At the same time, we have seen how feminine attributes can be so important for men to have a healthy and balanced life, and they should not be considered shameful or inappropriate as they usually are. The purpose of these principles is to uncover the unseen and lead us to a better version of ourselves, if not in terms of social norms, at least in terms of what makes us happy and authentic.

On your journey to make friends with your feminine aspect, you will discover how valuing and nurturing only a few of these principles is enough to eventually lead to a healthy expression of the other principles as well, since this energy is cohesive and cannot be divided. So if you feel that you do not resonate or do not fully understand some of them, you can always choose to focus on the others. Actually, just adhering to two or three of them is enough to witness your feminine energy growing. There are many different feminine archetypes and not one expresses all of these principles at once, but rather focuses on a few of them (like for instance Aphrodite, the goddess of love and beauty, who chose to focus on these two). The perfect embodiment of all feminine principles does not exist in the real world, nor is there a necessity for it, since we are here to learn from each other and complete each other. Completing does not mean that we are not whole within ourselves because we do not express a certain attribute in an obvious way, but rather that there is an opportunity to witness it in other people and learn from them. It is actually useful to give it a thought and identify which of these aspects come more natural to you and to cherish them, but also identify which are more challenging because they represent your best opportunity for growth.

These principles can also shed some light on the way we choose our partnerships, since two people who express different archetypes will unconsciously tend to choose one another. Opposites attract, regardless of the type of partnership and of gender. Sometimes, these relationships prove to be more intense and dramatic than the ones between two very similar people, but they are also the ones that help us evolve most and become more understanding of life itself.

Also of note would be that feminine energy is very ethereal and spiritual per se, so one cannot speak about the feminine in physical terms; the physical has very little to do with it. Not being aware that there are other subtler ways of expressing it (and much more powerful for that matter) leads to young women feeling pressured to look and behave in a certain way, and to men feeling a sense of obligation to inhibit it altogether. This is why education on what feminine or masculine energy actually means, is so important in this day and age in young people, but also at a later stage in life, since the journey of self-discovery and learning never ends. Because feminine energy is all about the inside and not about the outside, it can help with unveiling parts of ourselves which we were not aware of, and this process is always exciting and rewarding.

In the hope that you have found this book both educational and entertaining, and that you have discovered at least a few aspects to take away and use on your path of self-improvement or spiritual awakening, I wish you a most inspiring and joyful journey ahead.

O-BOOKS

SPIRITUALITY

O is a symbol of the world, of oneness and unity; this eye represents knowledge and insight. We publish titles on general spirituality and living a spiritual life. We aim to inform and help you on your own journey in this life.
If you have enjoyed this book, why not tell other readers by posting a review on your preferred book site?

Recent bestsellers from O-Books are:

Heart of Tantric Sex
Diana Richardson
Revealing Eastern secrets of deep love and intimacy to Western couples.
Paperback: 978-1-90381-637-0 ebook: 978-1-84694-637-0

Crystal Prescriptions
The A-Z guide to over 1,200 symptoms and their healing crystals
Judy Hall
The first in the popular series of eight books, this handy little guide is packed as tight as a pill-bottle with crystal remedies for ailments.
Paperback: 978-1-90504-740-6 ebook: 978-1-84694-629-5

Take Me To Truth
Undoing the Ego
Nouk Sanchez, Tomas Vieira
The best-selling step-by-step book on shedding the Ego, using the
teachings of *A Course In Miracles*.
Paperback: 978-1-84694-050-7 ebook: 978-1-84694-654-7

The 7 Myths about Love...Actually!
The Journey from your HEAD to the HEART of your SOUL
Mike George
Smashes all the myths about LOVE.
Paperback: 978-1-84694-288-4 ebook: 978-1-84694-682-0

The Holy Spirit's Interpretation of the New Testament
A Course in Understanding and Acceptance
Regina Dawn Akers
Following on from the strength of *A Course In Miracles*, NTI
teaches us how to experience the love and oneness of God.
Paperback: 978-1-84694-085-9 ebook: 978-1-78099-083-5

The Message of A Course In Miracles
A translation of the Text in plain language
Elizabeth A. Cronkhite
A translation of *A Course In Miracles* into plain, everyday
language for anyone seeking inner peace. The companion
volume, *Practicing A Course In Miracles*, offers practical lessons
and mentoring.
Paperback: 978-1-84694-319-5 ebook: 978-1-84694-642-4

Your Simple Path
Find Happiness in every step
Ian Tucker
A guide to helping us reconnect with what is really important in
our lives.
Paperback: 978-1-78279-349-6 ebook: 978-1-78279-348-9

365 Days of Wisdom
Daily Messages To Inspire You Through The Year
Dadi Janki
Daily messages which cool the mind, warm the heart and guide
you along your journey.
Paperback: 978-1-84694-863-3 ebook: 978-1-84694-864-0

Body of Wisdom
Women's Spiritual Power and How it Serves
Hilary Hart
Bringing together the dreams and experiences of women across
the world with today's most visionary spiritual teachers.
Paperback: 978-1-78099-696-7 ebook: 978-1-78099-695-0

Dying to Be Free
From Enforced Secrecy to Near Death to True Transformation
Hannah Robinson
After an unexpected accident and near-death experience, Hannah
Robinson found herself radically transforming her life, while a
remarkable new insight altered her relationship with her father, a
practising Catholic priest.
Paperback: 978-1-78535-254-6 ebook: 978-1-78535-255-3

The Ecology of the Soul
A Manual of Peace, Power and Personal Growth for Real People
in the Real World
Aidan Walker
Balance your own inner Ecology of the Soul to regain your
natural state of peace, power and wellbeing.
Paperback: 978-1-78279-850-7 ebook: 978-1-78279-849-1

Not I, Not other than I
The Life and Teachings of Russel Williams
Steve Taylor, Russel Williams
The miraculous life and inspiring teachings of one of the World's
greatest living Sages.
Paperback: 978-1-78279-729-6 ebook: 978-1-78279-728-9

On the Other Side of Love
A woman's unconventional journey towards wisdom
Muriel Maufroy
When life has lost all meaning, what do you do?
Paperback: 978-1-78535-281-2 ebook: 978-1-78535-282-9

Practicing A Course In Miracles
A translation of the Workbook in plain language, with
mentor's notes
Elizabeth A. Cronkhite
The practical second and third volumes of The Plain-Language
A Course In Miracles.
Paperback: 978-1-84694-403-1 ebook: 978-1-78099-072-9

Quantum Bliss
The Quantum Mechanics of Happiness, Abundance, and Health
George S. Mentz
Quantum Bliss is the breakthrough summary of success and spirituality secrets that customers have been waiting for.
Paperback: 978-1-78535-203-4 ebook: 978-1-78535-204-1

The Upside Down Mountain
Mags MacKean
A must-read for anyone weary of chasing success and happiness – one woman's inspirational journey swapping the uphill slog for the downhill slope.
Paperback: 978-1-78535-171-6 ebook: 978-1-78535-172-3

Your Personal Tuning Fork
The Endocrine System
Deborah Bates
Discover your body's health secret, the endocrine system, and 'twang' your way to sustainable health!
Paperback: 978-1-84694-503-8 ebook: 978-1-78099-697-4

Readers of ebooks can buy or view any of these bestsellers by clicking on the live link in the title. Most titles are published in paperback and as an ebook. Paperbacks are available in traditional bookshops. Both print and ebook formats are available online.
Find more titles and sign up to our readers' newsletter at http://www.johnhuntpublishing.com/mind-body-spirit
Follow us on Facebook at https://www.facebook.com/OBooks/
and Twitter at https://twitter.com/obooks